LEAP OF FAITH 2

If God had given me the opportunity to look across all of eternity and pick my parents, I *would* have selected Jean and David Rose. I'm so fortunate God chose them for me. They have been all I've ever wanted and all I'll ever need this side of Heaven.

I'm so happy the Lord has allowed me to live long enough to realize just what a treasure they are. Mom and Dad, thanks for being not only my parents . . . but my friends, too.

I know that I am one of very few who get the chance to say, "Mom and Dad, you're the greatest! You've done everything right. I dedicate this book to both of you. I love and appreciate you guys more than you'll ever know."

Steve

P.S. Oh, and with this dedication, I mercifully forgive all your debt accrued with me. You know, from money you've borrowed over the years. Or was it the other way around?

LEAP OF FAITH 2

God Loves Packer Fans

Matt,

I pray the message of this book Blesses
you. All my
Best to you.

Steve Rose

[signature] Steve Rose

John 3:3

Fisk

11/9/97

Prairie Oak Press
Madison, Wisconsin

First edition, first printing
Copyright © 1997 by Steve Rose

Prairie Oak Press
821 Prospect Place
Madison, Wisconsin 53703

Typeset by Quick Quality Press, Madison, Wisconsin
Cover concept by Sherry Klinkner
Printed in the United States of America by Master Litho, Neenah, Wisconsin

Library of Congress Cataloging-in-Publication Data

Rose, Steve
    Leap of Faith 2: God loves Packer fans / Steve Rose. -- 1st ed.
       p.   cm.
    Sequel to : Leap of Faith : God must be a Packer fan.
    ISBN 1-879483-46-7 (cloth : alk. paper). -- ISBN 1-879483-47-5
(pbk. : alk. paper)
    I. Green Bay Packers (Football team)   2. Sports--Wisconsin--Green
Bay--Religious aspects.   3. Football players--Wisconsin--Green Bay--
Religious life.   4. Football fans--Wisconsin--Green Bay.
I. Title.
GV956.G7R67   1997
796.332'64'0977561--dc21   97-37794
                                                               CIP

CONTENTS

FOREWORD

By Ken Ruettgers

U•nique (yoo-nek') adj. 1. Being the only one of its kind. 2. Without an equal or equivalent; unparalleled. 3.a. Characteristic of a particular category, condition, or locality. b. informal. Unusual; extraordinary! (exclamation is mine!)

From the beginning of my NFL journey, my perspective of Green Bay—the community, the people, and the love affair between the fans and the Green Bay Packer players and organization—can be summed up in a word: UNIQUE!

There is no other NFL community like Green Bay, Wisconsin; it's "the only one of its kind." The quality and character of the Green Bay Packer organization, administration, and players is "without an equal or equivalent; unparalleled." The relationship enjoyed between the fans and their team is far beyond any "characteristics of a particular category, condition, or locality." And when you put the entire Packer package together you have much more than "unusual." You have "Extraordinary!" You have unique.

What other professional sports franchise has 32,000 fans on a waiting list for season tickets? (A turnover of six tickets is projected for the coming season.) How about a Super Bowl victory parade with more fans in attendance than the population of the NFL franchise city? Incredible! Those are more than numbers; they represent the hearts and passions of the people that make up those numbers. You can see the unique relationship between the fans and the Packers in other areas too. You won't see other pro athletes in their franchise cities sharing bicycle rides to and from training camp practices with neighborhood kids. Or the "Lambeau leap" made famous by the Packers. How about the thousands of fans who wait hours at the airport for their team to return home—win or lose? Unique? You betcha!

With the average career length of less than four years, twelve years is a long time to spend with one NFL franchise, especially in this modern era of free agency where players and teams play musical chairs. Looking back without regrets, I wouldn't change a thing in my twelve years with the Green Bay Packers. That could be hard to say for a guy that spent his first twenty-two years in sunny Southern California only to be drafted onto the frozen Green Bay tundra spending the next five NFL seasons winless. But hard work and patience has been rewarding and encouraging for me and my family as we have become adopted citizens of the Green Bay Packer community. We are proud Cheesehead family members along with the many other hundreds of thousands of Packer family members that have embraced the players.

My wife Sheryl and I, and our children, have been uniquely blessed by the warm and friendly people of this community who have received us into their fold. The Packer experience is a unique NFL experience from a player's perspective. I could recount dozens of stories about the extra special relationships that have warmed the hearts of my family and forged a relationship with this wonderful community.

From the beginning through the end of my career, and now beyond, the personal support from the organization, fans, and community have been unique. As the door closed on my NFL career my wife and I were overwhelmed by the support, prayers, and good wishes. Via fax, mail, phone, in person, and by petition it has been a loud cry that has rung in our minds and hearts: "only in Green Bay, Wisconsin!" There is no doubt that my Packer experience has been unique from beginning to end. I am thankful to the community and fans and humbly go on record here: "Thank you for your overwhelming and unique support!" Only in Green Bay! It has also been a unique blessing to return the interactive blessings and give back to the Wisconsin communities.

My last duty as a Green Bay Packer was to receive a Super Bowl ring as a guest during the ring ceremony at the Oneida Riding and Country Club on June 4, 1997. I can't dream of a better way to close the chapter on 12 years as a Green Bay Packer in the NFL. I have had more fun as a Packer than a guy should be allowed to have. I couldn't dream up a better ending to a Cinderella saga.

The Packer organization continues to improve as a quality outfit. I am thankful for Bob Harlan, Ron Wolf, Mike Holmgren, and the rest of the members, staff, and players in the Packer organization. The last five years have been the best. In life you cross paths with quality character people—unique individuals—and it has been "beyond words" to cross paths with these fine people and spend time working with them towards common goals. It has been great to be part of a heritage-rich organization. I am thankful for being a small part of its history and for being part of this modern-day turnaround and success story that has brought back glory and victory to Packer fans everywhere.

What has been truly unique about the resurgence to Packer glory and the Super Bowl is the inside story that you won't read about or hear about in the mainstream media. Let's face it, most guys are guarded around the Green Bay and Wisconsin press and leery of being taken out of context or misrepresented. You rarely get the real story. And you almost never get below the surface.

Providing an avenue for allowing my teammates to talk vulnerably and honestly in an uncensored platform began in 1994 on the airwaves of WORQ's sports radio segment "The Timeout Show" with Steve Rose as my co-host. Listeners were encouraged, moved, and deeply touched by the player interviews. The player guests, teammates willing to give back uncensored to the fans, enjoyed talking freely about their faith and team interaction and behind the scenes. This is what spawned the uncensored relationship between Steve and the believers on the team. It was also a good excuse to get together over lunch and ice cream.

In Steve Rose's first book, *Leap of Faith: God Must be a Packer Fan*, Steve scored a touchdown by providing the same vulnerability and open honesty that was present on the "Timeout" radio show. The feedback that I have received from Steve's first book has been overwhelmingly positive. It seems that almost everywhere I go people are raving about *Leap*.

In this, Steve Rose's second book, what you'll get is far beyond what you'll read anywhere else. It picks up where the first book ends and takes you to new Super Bowl levels. Steve gives the reader a unique perspective that delves below the surface and is a springboard that allows you to leap into the hearts, minds, and souls of the Packer players from a locker room perspective. Steve has a special relationship with the players that allows them to be vulnerable and unguarded about the truth and their relationship with God. A player's perspective is that Steve is not a fan, not a player, but a bridge that closes the gap in a unique relationship between Packer players and their fans. You'll get a chance to be up close and personal as never before. You'll experience locker room camaraderie that goes beyond a sports journalist's filtered perspective and the biased self-perspective of the athlete-author.

I encourage you to take this leap of faith and dive into this unique perspective that only Steve can provide.

Best wishes and many blessings,

Ken Ruettgers

ACKNOWLEDGMENTS

First and foremost, thanks to my Lord and Savior, Jesus Christ, for a second chance in life. Truth be known, I should be dead, but You have given me the renewing breath of Your spirit.

Once again, to my family, thanks for all your fuss made over me. You guys know how to make your son, brother, and uncle feel good. Special mention to my brother, Dale, and sister-in-law, Mary, for their impressive sales numbers with my first book! Keep up the good work. You're on top of my Christmas list.

To Pastor Bill Myers from my home church, Assembly of God, in Appleton, Wisconsin; you're precious. Thanks for preparing me for this voyage and praying me through it. Your passion to serve the Lord and win the world to Christ moves me. The devil's not real thrilled with us, I'm sure. Pastor, thanks for shedding light on the truth, that Christ is calling everyone from the darkness into His marvelous light.

To Vic Eliason and the great folks at the VCY America Network, well, you're just the greatest. I can't believe how good you've been to me as I've tried to juggle so many things. Your Christ-like walk and talk are very congruent. I have never been associated with a greater number of people of God, than all of you.

To my right hand man, Mike Utech, my Colonel Parker, thanks for splitting yourself in two for me. You are not only a good idea man and servant, but you are a greater person. Thanks.

To Bob Gardinier: Thanks for the accountability and the challenge to take my relationship with God to the next level.

Brad Vivoda, you are such an inspiration. Your timely words, and undying devotion to see and help me grow is appreciated so much.

One more time, my love and admiration to two of the warmest human beings I've ever known, Ken Ruettgers and Robert Brooks. I was just one of a couple million baffled Packer fans who had to ask, "Why couldn't you guys play in the Super Bowl?" It hardly seemed fair. But both of you know the trophy awaiting in Heaven is even greater. Thanks for being my friend and for the support of my ministry.

To everyone at home in Eden and Campbellsport—you're Super. Another big thanks to Jerry Ninneman at the *Campellsport News*. Nobody has been a bigger help . . . and you know I can use all the help I can get!

Thanks to Diane and Julie at the Neenah Post Office, and Jenni and Misty from Image Pros who have had to put up with me. You're more special to me than you'll ever know.

Thanks to Jerry Minnich from Prairie Oak Press. What a gracious professional you are. Are you sure you know what you have gotten yourself into working with me? Thank you, Jerry.

To all the bookstores, pastors, and school principals who invited me to come and see and talk with them, thank you. I can't wait to do it all over again.

To the hundreds of media people who stepped out with a leap of faith and have not only touched but grabbed onto this material, which can be pretty unpopular in some quarters, God has told me he is going to bestow a blessing on you. Be sure to share it with me when it happens.

To all of you who provided the hundreds of calls and letters, I hope we can see you down the road, either for the first time, or for the second or third. Thanks for being a part of the miracle. God bless you.

Steve Rose

Is This Packer Pen a Sword?

My fear as I penned my first book, *Leap of Faith: God Must Be A Packer Fan*, was that most of the words in it were mine. I thought that, if I had written it, how could it possibly have an impact on others? Thank goodness, my fears were not realized. The book *did* have an impact—and I praise the Lord for that. I hope that this one will have an impact, too.

Leap of Faith: God Must Be A Packer Fan, was released on September 1, 1996. It was written a year before the Packers won Super Bowl XXXI. However, we didn't need a Super Bowl victory to be convinced that God blesses our beloved green and gold. Sure, God does bless Packer fans, but at the same time you'll never hear us say that the Vince Lombardi championship trophy in Green Bay means that God loves Packer fans any more than those of the Cowboys, or the Bears, or any other team.

Pastor Dan Ostrowski told me that only three percent of all books sell as many as five thousand copies. *Leap of Faith: God Must Be A Packer Fan* has sold nearly *forty thousand*, and that in only *five months*, and primarily in one state!

So what's the point? It is that the book's message must have been welcomed, that God has chosen to speak through a group of men who just happen to play football in Green Bay, Wisconsin.

I have computer discs to prove that I was the one who punched out the words to both manuscripts into a computer. But the testimonies of lives touched all over the country is enough to force me to divorce myself from acknowledging any responsibility for them. I cannot take any of the credit personally. Whether I'd like to is another story. After all, I'm only human.

So, then, who wrote these books if I did not?

I was asked many times during my first book tour, "Steve, did you have some help when you wrote your book?"

"Yes," I could reply, "it was ghostwritten. The Holy Ghost wrote the whole thing! I guess that makes it a Holy Ghostwritten book."

By now you may think, "Come on, just why do you really believe God's hand is in the writing of these books? Well, we have received numerous cards and calls to confirm this belief. But none confirms it more strongly than a letter we received three months after the book was published. It was from Hales Corners, Wisconsin, a suburb of Milwaukee. An obviously very intelligent lady by the name of Diane (I'll omit her last name to protect her privacy) wrote this to me:

> Steve,
>
> I wanted to send you a note first to let you know how much I enjoyed your book, *Leap of Faith: God Must Be A Packer Fan.* Second, I wanted you to know that I've taken that leap!
>
> I've always believed in God, but He really wasn't a part of my life. Your book has helped me see the light, so to speak.
>
> The next book that I'm reading is the Bible. Thank you so much!
>
> God Bless,
> Diane

Now, I can promise you that I can't make anyone want to read the Bible! Only the Lord can do that. Aside from the Bible, the book you are clutching may be one of the most important books you will ever read in your life! I can say that because I really do believe God wrote it! I promise, if you'll take the leap of faith that is woven into this book, your life will changed for the better—forever.

This book, and *Leap of Faith: God Must Be A Packer Fan*, are not the Bible, but they are alive! A lot of what God wanted me to tell you in the first book has either been enlightened over the past year or has literally come to fruition! Should we be surprised? No—because God is God!

Just as in *Leap of Faith: God Must Be A Packer Fan*, I know there are a couple things I *am* very certain God wants me to tell you. One is that He *does* love you. In this book, He has asked me to tell you why and how much. Secondly, He has told me to reveal to you the most important question you will ever be asked. I'll go as far as to say it's the only question that really matters. Watch and listen closely for it. Make sure you don't miss out by not reading on.

Last season, Reggie White said, "I've never tried to force my faith on anyone." And here in this book it's not my intention to force anything on you, either. Frankly, God doesn't force himself on anyone, including football teams. He will reveal himself to those who seek and honor Him. Is that you? If you choose to read this, I believe you'll find out why God does love Packer fans—fans like you. It's just a few hours of reading . . . and a leap of faith away!

Chapter 1

So, Is God a Packer Fan?

"**I**t was Jesus' plan. People all around the country can laugh all they want to, but I know what God said to me and it worked out that way. He wanted it to." Those words came from Reggie White of the Packers. What did he mean? Just what is Jesus' plan?

The Packers had just won the National Football Conference Championship over the Carolina Panthers, 30-13, when White made those bold comments. The gentle giant said God had brought him to Green Bay for a "higher" calling.

White knew that his moving, under free agency, from Philadelphia to the land of the frozen tundra was all part of a divine plan. "God sent me here," he told the media. And as badly as we wanted him and his Hall-of-Fame credentials clad in green and gold, we still had to ask ourselves, "Why would God send anyone to Green Bay?" After all, this was a team to which NFL coaches had previously threatened to trade players. The town was even referred to once as "Lower Siberia."

Let me ask you this: Where does it say in the Bible that God cares about football? Would He favor a certain team? Is there something supernatural going on here in Green Bay? Is there enough evidence to convict or anoint Reggie White of being an agent, vessel, and mouthpiece for the Lord, Jesus Christ?

The verdict is yours. Over the next pages we will present a case that may leave you with the same conclusion as White or leave you something of a skeptic.

In the first part of this Packer feel-good trilogy, many people thought I was a little goofy for going out on a spiritual limb to proclaim that "God Must Be A Packer Fan."

I first made this claim one year before the Packers won the Super Bowl! The Packers had just come off a another disappointing finish. Although we made it to the NFC Championship in 1995, it just didn't seem like enough. Again, we had lost twice, including the championship, to the same team. No hard feelings, but we won't mention their name or where they are from (those guys with stars on their helmets, you know, down in Texas).

So it wasn't as if we were trying to say that because the green and gold were world champs or something, that they were on the top of God's list. That wasn't the case at all. I believe, with Reggie White, Ken Ruettgers, and others that where God is given his place, he will move. In Green Bay, God is given his place and he is moving. It's that simple.

God says in His Word that He will use those who give Him honor. A number of Packer players from yesterday and today have chosen to spread God's word through love in action.

"Whoever has my commands and obeys them, he is the one who loves me. He who loves me will be loved by my Father, and I too will love him and show myself to him" (John 14:21 NIV).

Robert Brooks expressed these feelings in the foreword to my first book, *Leap of Faith: God Must Be a Packer Fan.* Here is what he said:

> Actually, it doesn't take a lot of faith to believe that God is the true leader of the Packers, which is just one of the issues in this book. Let me take you back a couple years and jog your memory.
>
> Did you notice the change that came to Green Bay right after we signed Reggie White? Besides bringing a great game of football to town, what else is his mission? Who is his leader? What really makes him tick and gives him purpose? His faith is in

the Lord, right? Doesn't it make sense miracles would follow him here?

I'll share with you that shortly after Reggie arrived in Green Bay he and Ken Ruettgers started an Accountability Bible Study Group on our team. Together, we sought God's will for the guys and our won lives. I agree with Ken Ruettgers when he said, "The miracles and other special things that have happened for the Packers are by-products of the faith of the players and the fans."

Today, these words certainly may have more credence. I think one oversight may be that the pendulum started to swing in 1992 when Holmgren came to town, but who's being particular? I am sure there are many still having some trouble buying into this whole program that God brought Coach Holmgren and Reggie to town. More than once, the play on words in the title *Leap of Faith: God Must Be A Packer Fan* stimulated some good conversation.

"So, do you really believe God is a Packer fan?" I'd be quizzed. Most of us Packer fans have little problem believing this to be the case. Many of the bleeding green and gold really just want a little more reinforcement for the notion. They've felt this to be the case for many years. But in Chicago? Well, let's just say it's a tougher sell there. We've never said the the Bears are the devil's team, just that God loves our Packers.

I celebrate with those who tip their hats to this team and can see that God is showing some favor while we leave the naysayers to stew a bit. Arguing solves nothing. In the book Proverbs it says, "Even a fool is considered wise when he shuts up." Besides when you roll around with a pig in the mud, you both get dirty—and only one of you likes it.

So is it God's blessing on the Green Bay Packers that makes them so warm, lovable, and easy for God to bless? If not, what do they possess that has quenched the thirst of their loyal fans, even during a twenty-nine-year drought? I think we have a better idea today than we once did just what it is about this team. Let's just say the picture has gotten a bit clearer.

Let me confess that, as I write with God's leading, if it sounds like I'm part owner of this team, it's because I am. And if you're a Packer fan, so are you! Joining us are a few million other Cheeseheads around the state of Wisconsin, the United States of America, and the world.

I will refer to the Packers as *my* team. So can you. You probably do anyway. We need offer no apology for this.

For the past four years God has given me the most wonderful view of what the Lord has been up to in the lives of some people who just happen to play professional football. The place they call their office is Lambeau Field. It's in a town many of us will claim is the floor below Heaven. We speak of our beloved Packers, their workplace in the city of Green Bay.

It seems like yesterday when I first saw the largest walking teddy bear I'd ever seen, lumbering towards me in the studios of "Q" 90.1 FM in Green Bay. His name was Ken Ruettgers and he turned out to be one of the most humble men I have ever met. Together, in 1994 and '95, we co-hosted the "Timeout" program. The show featured Ken's observations and those of many of the Christians on the team.

As these players came in to do the show, I kept hearing them say things like, "You know, we don't care who scores the touchdowns, we don't care who gets the glory on this team. All we care about is winning so that we can have more opportunities to be role models. We just want to win a Super Bowl so our platforms can be broadened."

What was a bit disturbing is that, even though I know they were saying the same things to the media outside the station, I wasn't reading their comments in the newspapers, hearing them on the radio, or seeing them spoken on TV. Why? Is the media more interested in yardage, sacks, and who is going to be the starting quarterback the upcoming week than they are in what Reggie calls the "big picture?"

No one knows more than the guys sharing their faith that the world is a tough place to minister to, but they aren't discouraged. Matter of fact, it's not even really about Super Bowl rings. The true reason why Reggie White wanted a Super Bowl ring was as clear as crystal.

"A Super Bowl win would give me a wider audience to preach to. It broadens my pulpit. So ministry-wise it's great. Ever since I was a kid, I've always wanted to be in a position like this to be a minister, to have an opportunity to have an impact on people's lives.

"It would be great to win a championship to get a ring," White adds. "But if I haven't impacted anyone's life, the ring on my finger means nothing. I want to love and touch people's lives."

Who is the only one who can make sixty thousand people stand and roar at the mention of Jesus Christ? It's Reggie White, either talking or singing. Where does this happen? In Green Bay, at Lambeau Field. What normally happens there? They play football.

In a hundred years, is it going to matter if the Packers played there? Is it going to matter whether they won Super Bowl XXXI? Probably not. Is it going to matter whether White shared the name of Christ there? Stay tuned.

Do you think God would favor these Packer players? Do you think God loves these fans, the same ones who are moved when they show "Amazing Grace" sung by White on the Jumbotron? Does the Lord inhabit the praises of his people as they cheer when it is through?

Friend, I can assure you if you will open your heart to the message God is trying to share with you at Lambeau Field, you will never look at this team the same way again. If you seek it, you'll enjoy a freshness and excitement like you have never experienced before. But only if you choose to "tune in" to what the Lord is saying through the team. Because it really isn't about football is it?

We have just scratched the surface of the real depth of the blessing that God wants to bestow on us. Friend, we may never win another Super Bowl in Green Bay again. Just how important is that anyway? Again, is it as necessary as catching the message God has for us through this team?

More answers are upcoming for you, a vital member of the contingent of the greatest fans in the world, Packer fans. And God does love Packer fans—just how much is an answer forthcoming, and one more leap of faith away.

Chapter 2

Love Affair at Lambeau Field

Who in the world would wait in a freezing cold parking lot to pay ten dollars for a box of dirt and grass? Who would call to pre-arrange their funeral and insist on getting a limited-edition, green-and-gold casket? Is there any doubt who these creatures are? None other than Green Bay Packer fans! Only Packer fans would do something like this.

In the off-season, thousands did buy pieces of the "frozen tundra" for charity. And they are reserving Packer-colored "used body cases" to take them away in style when their time finally comes.

It's hardly a secret that there *is* a love affair happening here. Even the boss will tell you. Packer president Bob Harlan says, "What is going on here is a love affair between the Packer fans and their team."

And after patiently living on memories of past glory days for thirty years, these fans, known around the world as "Cheeseheads," were finally rewarded with a win in Super Bowl XXXI. But a Super Bowl win wasn't necessary for the Packer fans to stick by their team. They have been some of the most loyal fans in sports history, through wins and losses. And there have been plenty of the latter in thirty years.

Michael Bauman, a sports columnist for the *Milwaukee Journal Sentinel*, has followed many sports franchises in his time. He makes some pretty strong statements about the love affair between the Packers and their fans.

He says, "Not only are they the best, there's no second place. Even during the long periods of struggle the seats have always been full.They are the most patient, loving, and kind fans you'll ever know. I am always astounded by the support of the team—win or lose."

Where does devotion like this come from? Why did Packer fans exercise this sort of patience to support a mediocre team, in a world where winning is everything, where folks jump off losing bandwagons like passengers on the Titanic? Is it the little brother thing the community feels as the David among the Goliaths of New York, Chicago, Dallas, and Los Angeles?

Maybe it's because fans feel they own the team, which in fact they do. The Green Bay Packers are the only publicly-owned franchise in the NFL. A total of 1,915 people currently own 4,634 shares of stock in the club.

Or is it because many of the special players on the team are worthy of such undying support?

In all my chats with many of the guys on the team over the last three years, it seems that the special situation with the Packers forces the players to be a part of the fans' extended family. It is in diametric opposition to the way fans in most large cities treat their teams. There's something different about Green Bay.

It's a wonderful love affair, but it also writes an unwritten condition into every Packer player's contract that he didn't bargain for. Just ask Brett Favre. A friend of mine, who owns a doughnut shop, tells me that Brett calls the shop ten minutes before he plans to come by. He orders a couple of jelly filleds. He then has to glide into the lot, hopefully unseen, send somebody in, and then make a quick getaway before he's recognized. The Packer fans' love can sometimes be invasive, even smothering.

It didn't take Eugene Robinson of the Pack long to realize there is something different about the fans here.

"The fans in Seattle were crazy, but they're crazier here," he said. "When Brett walked out for that Monday night game, that was the loudest ovation I've ever heard. They scream for everything—the fans here, wow, they really support you."

Peter King, from *Sports Illustrated* , told me, "In my thirteen years of covering the NFL I have never seen a player-fan bonding in sports like I've witnessed over the last two years." He went on to make this point which has been evident. "What is really amazing is that Packer fans are loyal regardless of the Packers' record."

The love affair went to the next level the day Robert Brooks first jumped into the Lambeau stands. It was in 1995 against the New York Giants. It was as if the lovable receiver was saying, "Hey, we love you as much as you love us. Here's a piece of me and us . . . we're yours."

Oh sure, it hasn't always been a bowl of cherries following the green and gold. Any Packer fan will tell you there is a discernable sense of a mood change in the community when the home team loses.

I recall my bride, Kim, reminding me how after a few losses during the Forrest Gregg days she'd say, "Steve, I can't look at you sideways without you getting snippy." I really couldn't see it then, but you know, maybe she had a point. I guess she *was* a walking matchstick, while I was sort of like a stick of gasoline-soaked dynamite. Of course, it wasn't my fault, it was the team's.

It's nothing to be proud of, but there is a rise in domestic violence calls to police in Wisconsin every time the Packers lose. That's pretty sad.

Radio broadcaster Gregg Owens is one of the patient diehards. "As the seconds ticked down in Super Bowl XXXI, I was numb! I didn't jump up or down or scream." Eventually, Gregg was able to let out his feelings.

"As Bob Harlan was accepting the Vince Lombardi trophy, I hugged my girlfriend Judi and started to cry. Twenty-nine years is a long time," he acknowledged.

One can ask, "Do we as fans take this love affair a little too seriously at times? Are we guilty of worshipping at the alter of green and gold? Has the pigskin become a golden calf?" A couple of Packer fans think so. Here are a few quotes from letters to publications around the dairy state.

"Too many of the fans treat attendance at a game like church. Their communion wine is beer and their communion wafer is a brat in a bun.

I know that may sound harsh, but it's true. I do consider myself a Packer fan in a big way," concluded B.G. from Appleton.

Esther, from Green Bay, challenged fellow Christians in *Together in Faith*, a Christian publication. She wrote this to fellow fans. "You are excited about the recent victory at the Super Bowl and that's great. But, are you as excited about the victory that is yours for eternity?" She wasn't through.

"Are you willing to spend the same amount of energy (and money) to help your neighbor make sure they have the opportunity to be sure of where they are going when the Packer victories have faded and death stands at the door?"

Pastor Paul Thierfelder, from Beautiful Savior Lutheran Church in Green Bay, regularly feeds the word of God to Packer fans. While preaching his children's sermon he reaches into a sack and pulls out a shiny stand with a tin foil-covered football on top.

"How many of you know what this is?" he asks.

"The Lombardi trophy," one youngster shot back.

"You have something more valuable than this—your faith in Jesus. We don't worship the Packers more than the Lord, but we like to ask the Lord to help them," he smiled.

A couple months after the 1997 Super Bowl, I was having lunch with Kenny Ruettgers, and he told me about his experience in the stands while watching the Packers in the NFC Championship. Lambeau had become somewhat of a sanctuary.

"They were playing 'Amazing Grace' on the Jumbotron. People were worshipping in a way I had never seen among Packer fans before.

Ken told me, "If that would have been church, I would have said, 'This is a little too charismatic for me.'" But he was also challenged by many of those people there.

"I had to ask myself, 'How is my expression of Christ being shown?' We're all fools for something . . . why not be a fool for Christ?"

One has to ask, "Where else is that gonna happen?" In all respect to Wrigley Field, the Boston Garden, and Dallas Stadium, I have never heard of a mini-revival breaking out during any of their games. Has God chosen Wisconsin, specifically Lambeau Field, as Reggie White suggests, to bring the message of His salvation here?

I will never forget January 27, 1997. It was the day after the Packers won the Super Bowl. I was heading up Highway 41, to Neenah. I looked into my rear-view mirror. Two out of every three cars must have had one of those Packer flags attached to their passenger window or radio antenna. Some had one on each side. They were headed to the "Return to Titletown" celebration to welcome the team home from New Orleans.

After running around the country for the past four months telling people not to put their faith in people, namely, football players, I felt there was something all right about the love for the team on this day.

A few hours later, I sat in the parking lot at Fox Point Plaza, waiting for an order of Chinese food to go, when I tuned my radio to the celebration going on at Lambeau Field. I couldn't help but think how nuts those people were. It was cold—very cold. As I sat there with goosebumps all over my body, I listened to the crowds roar its warmth and approval. And with every one of the players' words, I thought to myself, "Lord, *there is* something eternal about this day, but what is it? Please tell me."

A few days later, here is what I felt the Lord reveal to me in my spirit, which I need to share with you now. *It is simply that the bond between the Packers and their fans is one of the finest models we have for a true, pure, and loving relationship. You have the players who have told us we're the greatest. They jump into the stands to hug us. We love them through thick and thin, and they know that. It's a love affair, pure and simple.*

God wants you to know that we need to take this model of how a relationship should be and then take it into the schools, bring it into our homes, even take it into the church—that's right, even the church! Why are so many going to Lambeau Field? Is it because they feel loved there?

The Lord is showing me that it would be a great tragedy to leave this model of a loving relationship at Lambeau Field. Does that make sense? After all, why do we survive years of misery with the Packers, while, when a marriage gets a bit rocky, we want out in the first year?

Packer fans are even willing to sacrifice their summer. And in Wisconsin, the summer is really short. (Some say that it came on a Thursday last year.) WNAM-Radio's morning man, Ron Ross, explains:

"It's kind of strange. But in Wisconsin, we don't seem to mind how quickly summertime goes by because the end of summer means it's time for another Packer season!" You know, that's so true.

The cold can't penetrate the Packers or us fans, either. When it's ten below zero and the chill factor is thirty below, there's nowhere we'd rather be than bonded to a bench at Lambeau Field.

If allegiance can be metered by merchandise sales, then the Packers have one of the most explosive fan bases in sports history. According to NFL Properties, the Packers hit a record-setting $130 million in sales of Super Bowl XXXI merchandise. That's $30 million more than the previous record set when Dallas and Pittsburgh met in Super Bowl XXX.

Logo Athletic sold 650,000 of the Packer locker room hats that were given to Packer players and people in the organization after the game. That's 250,000 more than the previous high after the Chicago Bulls won the NBA title in 1996.

It gets crazier. NFL Films' Packer Highlights video sold more than 65,000 copies in its first five days and another 64,000 the next week. It is the fastest-selling video ever.

The NFL sold 950,000 Super Bowl programs, 250,000 more than the previous mark set when Chicago played New England in Super Bowl XX. There's some sort of noticeable allure to this team that's building in numbers and stature.

How many times have we heard people say, "Boy, if we could just transfer some of that love and enthusiasm, like our love for the Packers, to other things?" It's another slant on the old saying, "Why can't we keep Christmas in our hearts all year 'round?" I think that's what Kelly Roloff, from Stevens Point, meant in a letter to the *Stevens Point Journal* last January.

"Picture this," Roloff said. "A crowd of 60,000 excited Christians, donning hats, shirts, and jackets proclaiming their love for the Savior, hitting the streets for three hours on a sub-zero Sunday to share the Good News of salvation.

"Cameras pan the mass, revealing folks singing praises to God and exclaiming His greatness, excited believers offering prayer for the nation's leaders, youth, and schools."

Roloff concludes, "Wouldn't it be grand if we were so bold to witness that our commitment to Christ Jesus, the one Reggie talks about, were as visible as our fervor for the team?"

Can you picture this happening at Lambeau Field? Or is football all that should matter there? Fellow fan, I've learned that life insurance is good, but eternal life insurance, by trusting in Christ, is even better—and it's free. Salvation really is a super feeling. You're assured a victory, and the tickets have already been paid for.

I called the family funeral director last February, after the Super Bowl victory. I promptly ordered me one of those bright green and gold caskets. In commemoration of the Super Bowl, it was 31 percent off! Not only did I get a good deal, but the warranty says it has a lifetime guarantee!

Postcards from Training Camp

GREEN BAY, Wis.—Packers, Packers, Packers, Packers.

Don't think for a minute there's another sports team worth following or cultural event happening in northeast Wisconsin once the local football team commences training camp. Especially after its Super Bowl season. The two-a-day practices can draw crowds of 2,000. The autograph sessions afterward, featuring several players seated at a table and heavily armed with felt tip pens, cause long queues to form as early as 5 a.m.

"There's so much excitement from the Super Bowl hype of last year, and there's such a carry-over," rookie kicker Brett Conway says. "It's great to be part of it."

Crave more? Stop by The Packers Experience, with its interactive games, workouts and displays, through Aug. 3. And don't forget about the Packer Pro Shop with its array of merchandise, the Packer Hall of Fame and a tour of Lambeau Field.

Ah, Green Bay. The center of the football universe.

By Larry Weisman, *USA Today*

Chapter 3

Fond du Lac Here We Come!

It was 5:40 P.M. on September 16, 1996, as a gorgeous sunshine burst through the glass doors. I sank into the plush, soft chair in the middle of Robert Brooks' living room. The speedy receiver and I began a conversation. A wall separated the living room and Brooks first-floor bedroom. We began a conversation through it as Brooks changed clothes.

"How is the book doing?" he yelled to me.

"Great, just like you said it would, brother."

The Packer receiver was inquiring about the book for which the Lord had given me the words, *Leap of Faith: God Must Be a Packer Fan.* Just three months earlier Robert had written in the foreword that he had "seen the book's success already."

We were pumped. A limo was waiting outside to take us to the Ramada Ballroom in beautiful downtown Fond du Lac, Wisconsin. There we were going to kick off the *Leap of Faith* book tour with a signing. It was an especially big night for me going back home to Fond du Lac.

About three minutes later, Robert glided briskly through the spacious room and into his bright kitchen. He was wearing blue jeans, boots, and a casual long-sleeve shirt. On his head was one of his trademark Nike berets. He pulled some leftovers from the fridge and slid them into the microwave.

"I gotta eat something before we go, man."

He noticed that I was wearing gray slacks and a polo shirt. Robert took a glance at me and felt a little underdressed. Like my friend, former Packer Ken Ruettgers, I'm basically a T-shirt-and-jeans guy, but for tonight I was going all out.

As he disappeared again he asked, "Who's out in the limo?"

"Just the driver and her sister," I informed him.

"Tell them to come in."

I pulled the gold door handle of the limo and yelled, "Hey, you guys, come on in!"

Now Brooks emerged in an impressive dark short-sleeve shirt and tan slacks.

"Robert, meet Nancy and Tracy."

"How you guys doin?"

"Great," echoed the star-struck gals as they hugged God's gift to the front rows in Lambeau Field. The two classy ladies reacted as though they had just been introduced to someone they'd always wanted to have escort them to the high school prom. They looked awfully weak in the knees.

"Steve, why don't you show them the place while I eat?"

Down the stairs we went to the lower level.

"Here is where Robert recorded his song, 'Jump,' I told them. It was the single he released on compact disc that emphasized the love affair between Packer players and fans.

"Here's where you can watch Robert's wall," I joked. Whereas many people have a big-screen TV or an entertainment center, Robert has a big projection screen on the wall.

Back upstairs we played with Pocky, Robert's parakeet, as Brooks gulped down some nourishment. Robert's friend, Eric Baylor, was heading out the door to load the limo with some of Robert's CDs that he would sell for Brooks that night.

"You ain't gonna make me speak tonight are you?" smiled Brooks

"Darn right I am!" I assured him.

"He thinks I'm serious," smirked Robert to the ladies.

"How we doing on time?" I asked Tracy.

"We have time for a couple pictures and then we better fly."

We posed with Pocky and ten minutes later we were breezing down Highway 41 on the seventy-mile trip to Fond du Lac. Tracy drove, Robert was reading a manual about the keyboard he plays, and Eric was catching some zees.

"Does anybody want a soft-drink or juice?" asked Nancy.

"Can I get an orange juice?" asked Robert.

"I'll have diet, Nancy." Eric never moved.

I reached into this huge bag of popcorn, spilling two or three kernels, as I thought how this signing stuff was old hat for the Lambeau Leaper, while I wasn't quite so cool. I felt like there were a bunch of little people with feathers tickling the inside of my stomach. I was perched on the doorstep of my dream in which there was the fruition of God's vision for me with this book. God had given me every word of it.

"What are you doing on your day off tomorrow?" I asked Brooks.

"Flying to New Orleans."

"What for?"

"A commercial."

Robert is always on the go, and here I was on my way back home with him. Not just my friend, but a friend of everyone in the state of Wisconsin and many all over the United States of America, and Packer fans throughout the world. Many had fallen for him, from those who embraced him into their hearts as he launched into their homes through television, to those he had reached out to hug in the front rows of Lambeau Field.

Like a hot knife through butter, Tracy slid us through heavy traffic until a short time later we were pulling off on Exit 23 in Fondy.

"Nancy, can you get Mike Utech on the cellular? We need to tell him where we are," I said.

"Sure," she answered softly.

Mike Utech is my publicist and right-hand man in the Winners Success Network, my personal development company. He is also a master in setting up public events. He had coordinated the evening along with WTCX/WFDL Radio. He was amidst the commotion as Packer fans were flowing into the elegant ballroom in downtown Fond du Lac. I could barely hear him as we talked.

"Mike, we're just past Schreiner's [a popular restaurant]. How's it going?"

He had trouble speaking over the crowd. It sounded like halftime at the concession stand in Green Bay.

"There has been a steady line of people coming in for the last half hour and I think we're going to have to bring you in a different way."

The original plan was for Robert and me to come in the front doors, go up the stairs, and through the crowd. There was no way it was going to work, according to Utech.

"You're not going to be able to get through the crowd. It's too thick. The room is already full and we still have a line that goes out into the hall, down the stairs, and into the front lobby."

I know of only two people whom I have never seen become unglued in any situation—my brother Dan, and Mike Utech. Most people would have come undone, but not Mike.

"Steve, listen to me, there's an access door next to the head table. Tell Tracy to come in on Johnson Street past Main, then take a right on Macy. A crew is waiting to direct you into the parking lot, then to the ballroom from there. It's the only way we can avoid the congestion out front and in the building, OK?"

"Gotcha, Mike, see you in about five minutes."

About ten people from the radio stations were there to meet us. They had helped to sponsor the event. Tracy came around from the driver's side and opened the door and let us out. Greg Stensland, the news guy from the stations, was the first to greet Brooks. (Ironically, he had greeted Ken Ruettgers and me when were in Fond du Lac the previous April.)

"Robert, can you answer a few questions?"

"Yeah."

It felt like an eternity, but was only about two minutes later when Greg thanked Robert for his time. Jim Barnes, an old friend of mine, now a Fond du Lac radio personality, was one of the many who escorted us up the stairs. My heart was beating so loud, I was sure they could hear it inside.

When we finally got to the room, I saw and felt something like I never have before. It will remain locked in the caverns of my memory forever. From about fifteen feet away I saw John Gillespe, from the Rawhide Boys Ranch, who had graciously helped me in building Chapter 7 of the book. Behind him were six hundred people lined up like sardines in a room that was only supposed to hold four hundred!

Robert was to my left as we entered the southwest corner of the ballroom. In the twinkling of an eye the dimness turned to bright light. It felt as if we had entered a blast furnace. The room erupted into a thick, loving ovation. I am not exaggerating in saying that President Clinton would not have gotten the reception Robert did. Hey, I was along for the ride, and what a ride it was going to be!

Tom Biolo and Terry Davis, general managers from the stations, were there to greet us.

"Wow, great work, you guys, this is wonderful!" I said as I shook their and Mike Utech's hands.

I leaned to Utech and said, "Great job, Michael."

He graciously extended his hand towards the steps to the platform. I went up ahead of Robert. I should have let Brooks go first, but I was floating. I felt like a wet baby. You couldn't tell it from the outside, but it was a real warm feeling on the inside! I'm sure the instant replay will show that my feet were not touching the ground. Waiting on the top steps, four feet up, was my brother Gary, who shook my hand. He would accompany Robert at the head table for the signing.

"Robert," he said, "I'm Gary, Steve's brother, but please don't hold that against me." Brooks smiled. Just then Brooks was able to tell that my brother's sense of humor is crazier than mine.

As Robert and I sat down I gazed over the crowd to see whom I could recognize. There was my sister-in-law Shirley. I waved to Dan Fabisiak, Gregg Owens, Uncle Vic, and Aunt Jean. I sat looking out over the smiling faces while the faithful eagerly anticipated Robert's words and his autograph.

Tom Biolo, the master of ceremonies, introduced me to the crowd who looked as if they had been drinking coffee all day.

"I have to tell you this has been quite a day for me. I have thought of nothing else but being with you here tonight. My day has had no real sense of normalcy. I was in the shower for about thirty seconds before I realized I still had my glasses on," I said.

"Hi, Emily," I cried out. She was from Reach Out Books, a Christian bookstore in town.

I wasted no time in bringing my friend, the one everyone had come to see, to the lectern. "It is with great pleasure that I bring with me the most lovable, huggable man you would ever want to meet . . .

ladies and gentlemen, I give you number 87 of the Green Bay Packers, Robert Brooks!"

The crowd erupted again.

"It is a real joy to be with you here in Fond du Lac tonight. Steve says he's from here, is that right?"

They actually admitted I was.

As the crowd quieted, Robert went on to explain to them why he had made the trip this beautiful late summer evening.

"It was back in March when Steve and I talked on the phone. I called him from Phoenix. Early in our conversation I found out he was in Oshkosh writing a book while I was writing a song. Both were really about the same thing, the love affair between the Green Bay Packers and their fans," said Brooks with conviction. The room was very quiet.

He continued to build his case. "Furthermore, we both firmly believe that the hand of God is on this team. I need to give God all the credit for my success and I know Steve wants you to know that God has given him the words to this book. Thank you so much for coming out tonight. Have a great time," he said as he waved and they cheered.

Instructions were given as to how the one-hour signing would proceed. Robert stayed at the head table while a booth was set up for me just below and to Robert's left. This allowed the Brooks ticket holders to get a book and have it signed by me on their way to Robert.

I hugged my bookkeeper, Pat Bird, my personal assistant, Barb Nolte, and Julie Herzfeldt, from the Neenah post office. Julie is a Packer die-hard whom I'd asked to help at the event. She looked as if she was in Heaven. Her face just glowed. The series of clicks I heard were her camera. She caught the whole evening!

"Steve, how you doing, guy?" shouted a voice about ten feet to my left next to the line. It was James Breeden from Mount Washington, Kentucky. His wife, Ruth, and son, Pat, were there too. These people are Packer nuts, I'm telling you. They were featured in my first book in Chapter 13. Here, they were helping with crowd control. I'd invited Pat to ride back to Green Bay in the limo afterwards. He looked as if he, too, was in Heaven.

I began signing books feverishly. Larry Names, my editor, was on the way with more books. We could tell the supply we had was going to be dead in about forty-five minutes. Just to be sure, we asked the folks at Reach Out Christian Books to go and get some more. About five minutes later, I glanced over my shoulder and spotted Larry holding his daughter, Teagen. They sat to my right. If Larry wasn't sure the manuscript he'd sifted, pruned, and molded was going to be a hit, I think he knew it now.

The devoted Packer fans were just great and coming from many different places in their lives. Up stepped Clarence Boyke, my dad's best friend. He is not only one of the nicest men you'd ever want to meet, but one of the finest dairy men in Fond du Lac County—and the world. Our family has enjoyed the privilege of spending time with Clarence and his wife Ginny over the years.

A year earlier, Clarence Boyke had been diagnosed with cancer. He'd been given only months to live. Here he was, a year later, on borrowed time—and he knew it. This night he was having a blast. He looked like a kid.

With a huge smile on his face he stood before me with his book opened to the title page. "Could I have the honor, young man, of your autograph in this book?" he asked. Just like Reggie White, Ken Ruettgers, and so many of the guys on the Packers, he had given me such a great gift, making me feel special. It was a thrill to sign his book.

"Thanks Clarence, God bless you," I remember saying as I stood to shake his hand. That thick grin stayed on his face as he passed me on his way to see Robert Brooks to get his signature.

There was absolute pandemonium at all the booths and, of course, especially up by Brooks at the head table. My brother had the toughest job of the whole bunch that night. Sitting to Brooks' left, he had to play the bad guy and keep the flow of people going through. Everyone understandably wanted to visit with Brooks. But with 260 autographs to sign and 25 pictures to be taken, it wasn't possible.

God was proud of these Packer fans this night. Six hundred people having a great time, respecting those around them. There was never anyone pushing, shoving, or getting out of line. As a rule, where you have people there are problems. Not here, and usually not with Packer fans.

I was feeling a love all over this place such as I hadn't felt in a long time when a voice leaned in from the center while I was signing a book and asked, "Steve, any chance we can get our books signed?"

It was Richard Boelter, Jr. His dad's touching story was in Chapter 9. Reggie had phoned Richard's dad during the playoffs the previous year, thus granting a wish for the man who was in his last days of a battle with leukemia. Mr. Boelter, at White's invitation, also accepted Christ as his Lord and Savior on his deathbed.

"Mike," I yelled over my shoulder. "Can you run all of the Boelter's books through?" He nodded in the affirmative.

It was on this night I would learn something very peculiar. Everyone seems to think that when you write a book, you lose your memory.

"Do you remember me?" asked a girl whom I recognized as one who had graduated a year after I did at Campbellsport High School.

"Robyn, how are you?" She looked a bit surprised that I had recognized her. She was Robyn Zielieke, now Robyn King.

Then I felt a peck on my cheek.

"Hi, Steven." Only one person can get away with calling me Steven. It was Mom. I stood and gave her a hug.

"I love you, Mom." I embraced Aunt Joyce, too, and said hello to Uncle Norb. Near the opening of the booth stood a tall, sophisticated-looking gentlemen trying to talk his way in. Julie had politely told him no.

With a smile, the man said, "Does it count if I'm Steve's dad?" Julie's face turned red.

"Mr. Rose, why didn't you tell me?" Dad just smiled. Like Reggie, Ken, Robert, and others, he's very modest. Just like his sons—at least four of them, but maybe not me.

"Wow, what a crowd!" he said, his eyes gleaming as he scanned the room. I think he was pretty proud. Then, a mini "Chicago Cubs fan therapy support group" broke out as Dad and Larry shared their affinity (or illness, I'm not sure) for the Cubs. All they needed was my wife, Kim, and they would have had half the Cubs fans in Fond du Lac in one place!

As I continued basking in the moment I wish could have lasted forever, I saw a gentlemen approach me whom I'd been looking to see. It was Tim McGray. There was his wife Cindy and their cute daughter, Alyssa. Tim had told me a few weeks earlier that a picture of Brooks with Alyssa would be the ultimate. She thinks Robert is the greatest.

"Follow me, you guys," I said, temporarily leaving a line of folks who had wanted me to devalue their books with my signature.

"Mike, take care of my friends. We need to get a picture of them with Robert."

"Will do," he promised. Ten minutes down the road there were the McGrays. They looked like they had just seen the Lord. Well, it wasn't that good, but until the second coming, it would do.

"Thanks, Steve," said Tim gratefully. The look on Alyssa's face was all the thanks I needed.

"My pleasure, pal." If there was one thing I wanted to make sure happened that night it was to get the McGrays their picture, especially for Alyssa. To keep me humble, Tim writes to me as Steven "The King" Rose. I get the message.

I looked at my watch. It was 8:10 P.M. We were supposed to be out of there and Brooks still had about twenty-five people to sign autographs for. I was done. As I stepped out of the booth I talked to Hope from WTCX and then Jesse from Waldenbooks. There was Emily whom I'd yelled out to before.

"Come to Gille's afterwards," I whispered to Emily. I had conspired to run Robert through the Fond du Lac drive-in where they have the greatest frozen custard turtle sundaes on the planet. It would turn out to be an empty promise as Brooks was too bushed to make it.

The crowd filtered out of the room until there were only about thirty folks left. Someone wanted to say "hi" to me. I had no idea who. As I walked across the room, there was a pretty blond whom I recognized in an instant as she flew around the corner of one of the booths.

"Do you remember me?" she quizzed.

"Connie, how could I ever forget you?" I told her as she hugged my neck. I felt seventeen again. It was Connie Rosenbaum. Today, she is Connie Weiland. I was a senior at Campbellsport High School when she was a freshmen, and although I had a steady girlfriend, I did have a massive crush on her. But I couldn't ever get her to pay any attention to me in Mrs. Wenzlaff's class.

"Steve, the limo's leaving," warned Utech from about twenty-five feet away. Eighteen years after high school Connie had at last given me the attention I was looking for. Praise God. My past said I should be dead or in prison and here I was being blessed by her and so many others.

"Connie, it was great to see you," I said as I squeezed her hand and pulled away.

"Let's go, partner," I gestured to Brooks as we were headed out, when somebody requested one last picture. Utech tried to stay outside of the shot, holding one last book for us to sign as Brooks and I posed with my dad.

The book Utech was holding for Brooks to sign was for his brother-in-law, David Wilke. This special Packer fan was prayerfully recovering from a liver transplant in Madison. God has brought him through triumphantly.

As Mike waited with the open book, Robert posed between my dad and me. Flash, flash, flash.

"Give my best to David, will you, Mike?" asked Brooks as he signed his name on the page with his foreword.

Utech nodded and then said, "It's a long ride home for you. Let's get you guys out of here," as he shielded Brooks and me from the remaining people.

Down the ramp we went. The white stretch beauty waited idling as Tracy stood with the door open for us. Brooks and I waved to the folks on the second floor of the ramp. Quickly Brooks hopped in. I wasn't in quite as much of a hurry. Matter of fact, I was going to soak up every last drop of this occasion. Utech piled books in the car and Eric Baylor threw a box of Brooks' CDs in alongside the books.

"Mike, you did a sensational job!" I said.

"I'll call you in the morning," he smiled.

I admit there was a huge sigh of relief as we motored swiftly down the street. We had pulled off the evening without a glitch

"Robert, you want to get an ice cream cone at Gille's?"

"No, I gotta get up too early for my flight to New Orleans."

"You sure?"

"Yeah, I'm beat, man, let's go home."

It didn't take me long to see that Brooks was totally drained and was going to be out soon. I had to take care of a couple of pieces of business.

"Here's just a couple books I need signed, Robert," I pleaded.

They were for Paul Hornung, the former Packer great, and for my wife, Kim. He wrote in Kim's book,

KIM,
God has blessed us both with Steve Rose. He's the greatest!
—Robert Brooks #87

Shortly after, Brooks was out like a light. Pat Breeden sat to my right and we chatted about the upcoming season as Brooks napped. Eric, who was kept hopping selling Robert's CD, was out, too. Nancy again sat between them. I could tell she was enjoying being around greatness, just like the rest of us.

"Tracy, you've done great!" I said through the opening in the window which separated us.

"Thank you," she smiled gratefully.

About thirty minutes into the ride home, Brooks awoke. Patrick spotted an opening as Brooks came alive, briefly. "Robert, do you really like to jump in the stands as much as it looks like?"

"It's great, man, just great," he said wearily. Within seconds, he was out again.

About 9:30 we pulled into Robert's driveway.

"Can I get a picture of us together, you guys?" I asked. We got the picture.

"Robert, call me soon. I'll keep you posted on what's happening with the book," I said as I hugged him. "Thanks for making this one of the great nights of my life."

"I had a good time, Steve." He disappeared along with Eric into his stately brick home.

Minutes later I was posing outside of the Breedens' Green Bay home for a picture with Pat.

"Thanks, Steve. This was awesome. I can't wait to tell my friends in Kentucky that I was in a limo with Robert Brooks. They won't believe it." He trotted away like a boy who'd just met a Green Bay Packer. That's right, he had!

Later, we pulled into the parking lot at Gulliver's in Neenah where the trip had started. We were all exhausted.

"Don't open the door," shouted Tracy. "Let me do that. It's part of my job." I didn't argue. The pampering didn't have to end anytime soon on my account. I got out and pressed a ten dollar bill in Tracy's hand. I hugged the ladies goodnight.

Clarence Boyke having his book signed by Steve.

The night was history. There's only one thing that would have made the night complete and that was if my "Packer monster" could have come along. But Kim had to get up early the next morning and passed.

"How was it?" Kim mumbled as I plopped down next to her.

"It was unbelievable, just unbelievable, Kim." I think she heard that and then was sighing softly back into a deep sleep.

As I lay awake with moonbeams glowing through the window, I thanked God for the opportunity I had been given that night. There is no way I could convince anyone I deserved it, but God is good and He chose to bless me that night—big time!! All my strength comes from Him and that night, along with Robert Brooks, I tried to spread his love to hundreds in Fond du Lac.

As I was about to slide into deep, sweet dreams, I thought to myself, "About the only thing that could top this would be a Super Bowl win."

Only God, who loves us Packer fans so dearly, knew we were just a few more prayers and months away from it. What a ride it was that night and what a ride the rest of the season would be. What a ride!

Author's Note: On Sunday morning, March 9, 1997, Clarence Boyke died. The night of the signing in Fond du Lac was the last time I saw him. He had not lost his battle with cancer. I believe God may have merely convinced him it was time to go. He chose to use his illness to build love in his family. I will forever be grateful for Mr. Boyke's kind words in Fond du Lac on September 16, 1996. In loving memory of Clarence, I dedicate this chapter to the Boyke family.

Chapter 4

Angels in the "Lambeau Zone"

It's Monday night, October 14, 1996. The world is tuned to ABC's Monday Night Football from Lambeau Field in Green Bay. It's the third quarter as the Pack trails the San Francisco 49ers by a score of 20-6. The green and gold is in real need of a miracle to turn things around. They are on the verge of one.

For a moment, imagine the Twilight Zone's Rod Serling standing on top of the scoreboard at Lambeau Field. He is in a suit and wearing a Packer necktie, stars twinkling above him. He begins to speak in his stoic voice from the classic '60s show.

"Welcome to a magical little stadium in a small village called Green Bay. Some may say the guardian angels that once roamed the frozen tundra here during the days of one Vincent T. Lombardi have left. However, there is one player tonight who may disagree with that assumption. Tonight, we will soon eavesdrop on a conversation in the front row of this splendid football sanctuary. In just a moment, a quarterback by the name of Brett Favre is going to throw a pass to one Mr. Don Beebe. This veteran of no less than four Super Bowls has seen everything . . . well . . . almost everything. But very shortly Don is going to see something, and hold a conversation that could only have occurred . . . in the "Lambeau Zone."

(The camera pulls away from Serling; he shrinks back as the scene focuses on Brett Favre and the Packers on the field.)

"Hut . . . hut . . . hut," shouts the NFL Most Valuable Player. Frank Winters thrusts the pigskin to him. Favre looks right and then spots Don Beebe to his left. Zing, he hits Beebe with a bullet and down falls the speedy receiver. But no one has touched him. A hand from a 49er reaches over to touch him, which would end the play. Not sure whether the play is over or not, Beebe springs to his feet and motors fifty-nine yards down the sideline and into the end zone.

"Touchdown," shouts the zebra (referee) who has just arrived behind him.

As is normal procedure in other NFL cities, on other teams, Don heads to the sidelines to exchange some high fives with team mates and coaches. But then he realizes that he is in Green Bay. It's "Lambeau leap" time! With a full head of steam, he races back into the end zone and as if on wings, he flies through the air.

Just two seconds later, he has found himself in the front row of the stands on the lap of a very pretty lady! Mark Chmura, Adam Timmerman, and some of the guys are patting his back and behind as the fans swallow him with hugs.

It is just then that Beebe notices something peculiar. Beebe has read in Steve Rose's book, *Leap of Faith: God Must Be A Packer Fan* that there are twenty thousand Packer fans on the season ticket waiting list. And he is very suspicious and curious as to why there is an empty seat to the left of the gorgeous beauty in front of him.

Her blue eyes sparkle like the diamonds in her earrings. The pearls around her neck are stunning. She is wearing a heavenly, pure white flowing dress. It has green and gold sequins on it. It ripples in the autumn breeze. She smells sweetly of perfume. And her golden blond hair is hidden by a foam Cheesehead! (I guess she must have looked like June Cleaver wearing a Cheesehead.)

Beebe just can't get that empty seat out of his mind. For some reason, somebody was being robbed of an opportunity to watch a good game. He can't help but begin a conversation with this lady.

"Ma'am, who is supposed to be in the seat next to you?"

"My husband," she says smiling with her hands on each side of his helmet.

"Where is he?"

With no hesitation she tells him, "He died." She is smiling at Beebe, even though she has just told him her husband has died!

Don gasped and then gave his condolences. But he wasn't finished quizzing her.

"That explains why that seat is empty, ma'am, but who belongs in the two seats to your right?"

"Oh—those are for my kids!"

"Where are they?" asked Beebe, again a little disturbed.

"At the funeral!" she roared with her head tilting back and her eyes penetrating Beebe.

Suddenly spooked by this lady, Don puts his jets in reverse and lands back on his feet on the turf. He turns to walk away. Still shuddering, he stops and glances back over his left shoulder. The lady is gone—poof—history. The empty seats, at least the ones he thought were empty, are now filled with faces he didn't see just seconds before.

"C'mon you guys, didn't you see her!" he pleads to his teammates. No one verified seeing or hearing anything. They thought his sighting and story was a gas.

"Don, I could believe the Dallas Cowboys are all choir boys before I could buy your story!" laughed Aaron Taylor.

"I didn't see anybody there," said Adam Timmerman with a sly smile on his lips. "Don may have been a little delirious from the sprint."

"I don't know if Beebe is starving for attention or what," said Edgar Bennett. "Maybe he had a bad pizza the night before, I don't know," laughed the running back in the post-game interviews.

Three hours after the 23-20 win, in the locker room, Beebe stares off into the distance. He is the only player there. An equipment person is picking up towels.

(The camera is pulling away from this scene. Rod Serling appears at a table in the middle of the Packer locker, just feet away from Beebe)

Serling begins, "What do *you* think? Was there an angel in the front row at this shrine on Lombardi Avenue? Was she the Roma Downey of Lambeau Field? Had she been sent to the 'Lambeau Zone' to tell us something about priorities? It's a story for your perusal and personal file, one presented to you tonight that could only be found . . . in the friendly confines of the 'Lambeau Zone.'"

(The screen fades to black)

This story would be funny if it weren't so close to truth! Too many of us know just how wild this "Packer thing" really is. From eight to eighty, few can escape the grip of the romantic pull from these green and gold angels whom the Lord has entrusted to speak to us. Can their attraction lead us to where we sometimes cross a line?

Does our allegiance to this team sometimes lead us to cross the line from healthy fanaticism to idolatry? Is it all our fault? These guys on the Packers are so special, almost irresistible.

But isn't it refreshing to know that these players we have embraced in Green Bay show a genuine reverence for the Lord? One has to admit that, if we're looking for role models, there are quite a few of them wearing Green Bay Packer uniforms.

Christ said that we would know those who belong to Him by their actions. It's called walking the walk instead of just talking the talk. Over the years God has sent many of his messengers to play in the sometimes cold confines of Lambeau Field. The many faces and places of ministry are not always in the most desirable of locations. Let's meet a couple of the angels from the "Lambeau Zone."

It's no secret that the former player for the Philadelphia Eagles and the Miami Dolphins thought it was a bit too cold in the "Lambeau Zone" for his liking. But after encouragement from Reggie White, with whom he had played in Philadelphia, and Mark Ingram, his teammate in Miami, he was persuaded that Green Bay was different.

"The playing conditions here are great. If you're gonna play football, this is the only place to be. And man, these fans are the greatest!" said the bundle of joy. But there was one activity that he didn't adopt in his short stint in Green Bay. After touchdowns he stayed grounded in the end zone. With him being such walking love, and presumably able to mount up with his wings, why didn't he, too, do the "Lambeau leap?" Here was his answer.

"Three reasons," he said. "One, age. I'm thirty-one years old." (Don't some of us really feel sorry for him? Oh to be thirty-one years old again, huh?) Try again, Keith.

He continued. "Two, you gotta understand, Brooks, Freeman, and Beebe, those guys are 185 pounds with rocks in their pockets. When they jump up into the stands, its safe—a party. Me, I'm 250. If I jump up there I'll kill somebody!"

I really think you're going to like his last answer.

"And three, I promised my mama long ago I'd give glory to Jesus with a prayer in the end zone after every touchdown."

Keith Jackson and so many of his teammates think it's cool to be a Christian. They can't wait to score so they can "take the knee" and give God the glory. Isn't it remarkable that two years ago, when the team was trying to bring Keith to Green Bay, we were told that Jackson was money-hungry? Let's ask this: If Keith Jackson really were money crazy he wouldn't have retired leaving close to a million dollars on the table, would he? Of course not.

Today, just as Jackson had done then, he is building the lives of kids through his P.A.R.K. ministry in Little Rock. It stands for Positive Atmosphere for Reaching Kids. Keith, we'll miss you, friend.

In 1995, Robert Brooks wanted everyone to know that "God Loves Packer Fans!" He'd been called to a unique ministry. One as chief on-field public relations spokesman for the Packers. He explains how it all came about.

"I just wanted to show the fans that we love them as much as they love us. I made up my mind I was going to jump into the stands after a score. I wanted to take the love of the Lord into the stands. And—I wanted to have people forget about Sterling Sharpe for just ten seconds!"

Sterling who?

Many remember Ken Ruettgers as a great left tackle for the Green Bay Packers. He was. He was an angel of protection for Brett Favre's blind side. But one of the things that was most impressive was his constant profession of his love for Christ and for his family. They went hand in hand.

In his 1995 book, *Home Field Advantage: A Dad's Guide to the Power of Role Modeling*, Ruettgers poured out the message God had given him. After an eye-opening experience in the locker room, he decided to take it upon himself like never before to be *the* role model for his kids.

As an angel for the Gospel, Ruettgers was known for sharing his faith when the opportunity presented itself. The six-foot-six, 292-pound man of faith never thought twice about the persecution that would come from his boldness.

There will be one less angel after the '96 season in the huddle in the "Lambeau Zone." Besides setting a great example for the fans, many of the Packers set great examples for their teammates. Sean Jones, who retired after the 1997 Super Bowl win, was well known for a team Thanksgiving ritual. The muscular defensive lineman for the Super Bowl champs has a very special tradition he has carried through his career and into Green Bay. It goes back to when he was in Los Angeles with the Raiders in 1984.

"It was Thanksgiving while I was out in L.A. during my first year with the Raiders. I didn't know what I was going to do," said Jones. "Howie Long says, 'Are you coming over to eat?' I didn't turn down the meal."

That's why in two previous seasons and in 1996, Jones, with the help of newcomer angel apprentice, Santana Dotson, invited several Packers over to the Jones house on Thanksgiving following the morning practice. It is an annual event Jones has attempted to host ever since leaving the Raiders.

"I want to make sure no player is forced to spend the day alone at home eating a frozen turkey TV dinner. I especially try to make sure the young guys have someplace to go," said Jones.

Reggie White appeared on ABC television's "Touched By An Angel." He stood and talked to a group of gymnasts, which included the petite Olympic heart-throb, Kari Strug.

"Be sure to be good people away from all the glitz. It's what's left after you are done competing that's important," he urged them during the program.

It's not hard for us Packer fans to believe that we have been blessed with a host of angels. But it is nearly incomprehensible for Packer fans to think about a former Chicago Bear being an angel! According to Mike Holmgren, that was the case on the 1996 team. It is even more unfathomable when we learn it's Jim McMahon!

During the Pack's stay in New Orleans, Coach Holmgren acknowledged that he had two voices at his disposal to relate their experiences of the "Big Dance." They were McMahon and Don Beebe. While

Holmgren was happy to have two Super Bowl veterans to turn to, he admitted that he could not have picked two more contrasting personalities to discuss the topic with his team.

"It's like having a little bad angel and a little good angel," said a smiling Holmgren as he pointed to each of his shoulders. "I've got McMahon on one side and Beebe on the other, so that covers most things," he joked. It's kind of like reading the Bible and the newspaper so you know what both sides are up to.

Beebe an angel? You bet. McMahon? Now that could only happen in the mysterious confines of the "Lambeau Zone!"

Chapter 5

Rise and "Jump" Again

Ever since I've known Robert Brooks he's had faith in the Lord. But during the 1996 season, God took him to an even higher level. The official captain of the "Lambeau leapers" will tell you he's not only celebrating rebirth through Christ these days, but he has a "born-again" right knee to boot.

I was having a devil of a time getting hold of Robert Brooks because his off-season travels after the Super Bowl kept him on the road nearly constantly. And my schedule wasn't any less hectic. So we were playing a lot of phone tag and I was concerned about sneaking the update of his miracle in this book.

On Thursday night, July 3, I had written deep into the wee hours at my office in Oshkosh. When I got home I was so tired I didn't even check my phone messages. About 5:00 A.M. I awoke and was staggering through the kitchen when I noticed the light on the answering machine. I reached over and slapped the button.

"Steve, it's Robert. It's Thursday night. Give me a call and leave a message when would be a good time to call you tomorrow on the Fourth of July. You ain't gonna believe what I have to tell you, man," said the positive one. I couldn't wait to hear about it. He'd definitely piqued my interest.

Steve Rose pointing to Robert Brooks' "born-again" knee (top left). Steve with Packer wide receiver Derrick Mayes (#80) (top right). Steve and Robert Brooks enjoy a laugh at Brooks' Green Bay home (bottom).

Later that morning I left him a message, and we managed to talk to each other about six o'clock the next night. It didn't take long for me to realize that God was up to something between us—again. Last year, Robert was writing a song at his Phoenix home about the love affair between the Packers and their fans when he called me, only to find that I was writing a book about the same thing!

Within a few months we were standing before the Wisconsin media doing a press conference announcing the release of the his CD single, "Jump," and my first book.

"When can we get together, my friend?"

"You wanna come up tomorrow?" he asked.

"Is three okay?" I inquired.

"Let's do it."

Again he reminded me that I wasn't going to believe what he had to share. Honestly, I've come to learn that nothing surprises me where Robert Brooks is concerned. As I hung up the phone I felt a blast from the Holy Spirit which told me that my visit with Brooks was going to have a big impact on Packer fans who read this book.

It was a beautiful Wisconsin afternoon as I rolled off the freeway to Green Bay from Neenah. At three o'clock sharp I pulled into Robert's driveway. I walked in the front door. Robert was to the right standing over the sink thawing whitefish, talking with two other men.

"Guys, this is Steve Rose, who wrote the book."

"Steve, good to meet you," they echoed in unison. I went around and shook their hands. After they left, I learned that one of the men was Emory Smith, Emmett Smith's brother. He had been sitting on the couch reading my book. The other was Robert's brother, Charlie, who later joined us at the table.

As I leaned on the counter getting some of the latest team hoopla and quizzing the Packer wide receiver, Brooks threw a banana, some milk, ice, and protein powder in a blender. It looked like a shake when it was done.

"You wanna try some, Steve?"

"Yeah, give me a taste." I don't like bananas, but it wasn't bad.

"Well, let's do it," Robert said, indicating he couldn't wait to give me the lowdown on what had happened over the last couple of months.

We sat in his huge living room facing each other. I told him to start from the beginning. He pulled forward in his chair with his hands folded. He hesitated, looked down, then looked me right square in the eyes and began to tell me this incredible news.

"Steve, I had a dream during the second week of the season. In the dream, God told me to get out of the middle of the road in my faith. He told me not to be lukewarm anymore, to be either hot or cold."

Brooks admitted to me that he felt in the past he'd put a bushel basket over his faith. Although he was reading the Word and praying, he felt he wasn't sharing his faith like he should have been. It didn't take long for me to find out that those days were now over.

He continued. "So, God showed me in a dream that I was not going to be finishing the season. I didn't know how or what, but I knew I wouldn't be. The funny thing about it is, I only told Eric [Robert Brooks' assistant] 'cause I had to tell somebody," he said.

"To confirm it later," I interrupted.

"Exactly," he reported. "I told him and I was pretty sure he thought I was crazy. So, what happened is, I started having those concussions." As you may recall, Brooks was knocked out cold in both the Tampa Bay and Seattle games. I was at both of those road games during the book tour. It was spooky.

"It ended up the San Francisco game would be the day. The day started out really weird. First of all, Brett, who is my next door neighbor, asked me for a ride to the game. That was really different."

Brooks had my attention. I had no clue where this was going to go next as he continued.

"As you know, it was that night—*boom!*—the first play of the game I get hurt. I was in the worst pain of my life and it dawned on me, this was it! My dream had come true. I knew the season was done, just like the Lord had revealed to me in my dream. As I lay there I asked God, 'What's next?'"

He continued. "God had also revealed to me in my dream that the setback was not going to be permanent and that I would play football again. Nothing would be taken away from me. In fact, I was going to go to another level. I was going to help others around me to strengthen their faith."

As Pepper Burruss and the staff attended to the wounded Brooks on that night, Brooks prayed—not for himself, but for his teammates! He had a special request for the doctors.

"I told them to get me off the field as quick as possible. I said, 'Don't let my teammates see me down, don't let them see me cry. I want them to see me smiling, giving them a thumbs up,'" he recalled. The national television audience saw just that. It was an act. He was in terrible pain but wouldn't let his teammates or the fans see it.

"They took me into the locker room and I'm experiencing the greatest pain I've ever felt. They're trying to get me some ice on my knee and the pain is so bad it was actually leaving my knee and going to my hands," recalled number 87. "It was kinda strange."

Then came the next step in the revelation process.

"As I was just about ready to pass out, God told me why He had allowed me to be injured. The message that I got, right then and there, was that God was going to use me to show people that during their time of tribulation, or when something is bearing down on them, that they need to handle it, like I was going to handle my situation."

He continued. "First, have faith in God. And then everything needs to be positive, nothing negative. In other words, the way that God was going to help me was the way others could be helped, too. And I was supposed to share this message with others."

I loved this. My faith was growing by the second. I can't begin to imagine how he was able to trust the Lord like this, but he did, and you really haven't heard anything yet. He sat back in his leather chair and leaned a little to his right.

"The night before I went into the hospital for the operation [Thursday, October 17] I'm lying at home talking to Eric. I'm on the same spot where I told him about my dream. He's sitting on the couch and I'm asking him if he remembers the dream.

"'Yeah, I do,' he told me," recalled Brooks.

That night, Robert went on to remind Eric that God had told him earlier, before the injury, that it was going to have a happy ending.

"Well, that same night, Steve Newman, the Packer chaplain, stopped over. It was kinda funny cause it was the first time he'd ever stopped over to my house."

"Robert, I have some Bible verses for you that will help you get through your surgery," said Newman.

"One of the verses was from II Corinthians 1:3. In that scripture it says, 'Blessed be God, even the Father of our Lord Jesus Christ, the Father of mercies, and the God of all comfort; Who comforteth us in all our tribulation, that we may be able to comfort them which are in any trouble, by the comfort wherewith we ourselves are comforted by God.'

· "Do you see the correlation there?" Robert asked me before continuing. "I jumped forward and looked and told him [the chaplain] that was the exact same reason God told me on Monday night why He had allowed me to be injured. I asked God that night what was next, He told me, and now He had confirmed it in scripture!"

Isn't it just like God, to have His Word confirm His purposes, and in this case, His dream for Robert Brooks? Robert knew it was a gift that God chose to reveal more of the mystery to him. He knew God didn't have to do that.

Brooks explained to me that he had some awful painful days after the surgery. Over time, things settled down a bit. Then Robert wanted to know what the doctor's prognosis was. He hadn't heard from God yet on this, so off he went to consult with Dr. Pat McKenzie.

"Doc, what's my situation, how long will I be out?" he asked. "At first, Pat was kind of reluctant to commit to any timeline, and I told him, 'Don't sugarcoat it. Tell me exactly what's wrong, I want to know. Based on your medical experience, let me know what's going on.'

"He looked at me then said, 'There's a great chance that you will never play football again. I think the rest of your life will be normal. You'll be able to walk normally and everything. But, knowing you, you'll heal fast. We'll just have to see.'"

Friend, before we let Robert continue, we need to let you know just how serious this injury was. Robert had severely damaged the following: The pateller tendon, the anterior cruciate ligament, the medial collateral, and the maniscus cartilage all were torn. And on top of that, he had chipped a bone off the side of his right knee. It was this last injury that the doctor thought would rule Robert out from ever returning to football.

Robert told me that they were afraid he wouldn't be able to stand the pain of the "bone on bone" if the supporting tissue didn't grow back right. Any single one of these injuries can, and has, ended football careers.

For instance, Brian Noble suffered just one of the injuries Brooks had suffered. It was during his last year as a Packer in 1993. When I was in Wausau last year doing a signing with Noble, I specifically remember him telling me, "I really doubt if Robert will ever be able to play again." I couldn't blame him for thinking this. He's been there. He knows what it's like to be a football casualty, and just like the rest of us, he didn't know what God was up to with Brooks.

"When I got home," Robert continued, "I took all the faith I had, and prayed that God would heal me. Based on my faith, I asked in the name of Jesus Christ to heal me. I woke up the next morning with the revelation from God that He *was* going to heal me! But, something told me to go to Reggie. I did and told him that God told me I was going to be healed."

White, as many of us remember, has experienced several healings of his own in his four years in Green Bay. It was a meeting that, in Brooks' mind, was the turning point of the whole matter.

I said, "Reggie, God told me I'm gonna be healed, but I need you to put your hands on my knee and rub that oil you have on my knee." This is the same oil White had used on his own hamstring in 1995. Brooks told of the next step. "We went into Pepper Burruss' office and White anointed my knee with the oil and put his hands on me. From that point on, I knew that God would heal me," recalled Brooks.

Now Brooks wanted to weigh what God had told him against what the doctor has said. And he knew whose opinion he was going to trust. But just to have some fun, he went to see Dr. McKenzie again and got his opinion.

"Doc, write down on paper exactly how many weeks you feel I will be on crutches, how long before you think I'll be running, and how long before I'll be back in uniform. And he did. Just as he had earlier, the doc told me there was a chance I'd never play again, but if I did, it would take a year and a half for the ligaments alone, so much time for this, so much time for that and the other stuff.

"I looked at him and said, 'I'll be back in half the time!' Steve, as we sit here today . . . it's about half that time! And right now, I could go out and play you a professional football game. I was just going on what Jesus Christ had told me."

You know something, it was the day after I talked to Robert that I read in the newspaper he'd passed his physical with the team!

Well folks, what do you think? Are you a believer? Robert wasn't finished. For me, Robert brought back memories of times when the media couldn't figure out how Reggie, Ken, and others had beaten the odds with serious injuries.

"Here I sit today—a miracle—and everybody is scratching their heads," said Robert. "And I'm telling them I was healed from the moment I came home from being with Reggie. All I had to do was trust Christ. It was done!" declared the Lambeau leaper. "God had mapped it out for me. Every step along the way, God revealed to me what was going to happen. I'm not surprised. As a believer in Jesus Christ, that's what my God promises He will do for me. It's in the Bible."

What's the verdict on this whole deal? Robert went on to explain further why he feels God had chosen to use his pain for God's gain. "He knows your heart. And He knew through my faith in Christ that I would be able to trust Him. He told me, 'You know I want to use you, but you need to start walking the walk instead of just talking the talk.' Now I'm to the point where I am on a whole new level spiritually."

Folks, when I met Robert Brooks early in 1996, he was a man of great faith, but let me tell you, this is a new man. He has had an awakening that bears paying attention to and following. His walk and his talk are congruent. He knows that football is just the platform. His mission and calling is Jesus Christ's leading for his life. He told me.

"So what, I didn't play in the Super Bowl, but that's peanuts compared to where I am with Jesus right now. It's nothing compared to the people who will come to the Lord. It's about me showing people that through Jesus Christ, anything can be accomplished. Even when the doctors say you can't play. You can do anything!"

"Preach it, brother," I yelled to him, looking at his brother, Charlie. "What do you think?" I asked Charlie with a smile in my spirit. "Should we call the people to come with the white jackets and take your little brother away?"

"Hey, I'm so proud of him. He's bringing the family together through Christ. The little rascal is going all out to show his faith," replied Charlie.

I said to Brooks, "Robert, you have to be excited about taking this message to the people. They need to hear it."

"Yeah, they may not be ready, Steve, but they need to hear it," he replied.

Robert then told me some more about how he'd reminded me in the foreword of the first book that they were going to win the Super

Bowl. "Remember, I told you in the first book that we were gonna win? God told me."

"I know," I admitted, laughing.

"He didn't say I was going to win it or that Brett was gonna win it, but that the Green Bay Packers were gonna win it. What's that tell you?"

I loved his next point. "God knew I knew that it's not about one guy. That's why I think He knew my heart and faith and said, 'This is My guy—and He chose me!' I have stacks and stacks of letters from people telling me that my story has helped them make it through."

With all of the prophecy and revelations from Brooks, I couldn't wait for him to give me a little insight on the upcoming season.

"So, what's gonna happen, brother?"

"Aw man, it's an automatic. I'm gonna get my chances, we're gonna do well. And let me tell you. God's got it all worked out. The first game of the season is Monday night football. The questions will come out, 'Is Robert Brooks back to form? Is he gonna be alright with the knee?' "

It was then that Robert Brooks filled my heart with joy when he made this prophetic statement. You will know if it came true, by the time this book hits the stands.

"After I play, I am gonna sit there by my locker and tell them, 'Jesus Christ is my Lord and Savior and I told you . . . I told you . . . none of you all wanna believe it, [the healing] but it's true.' And I'm not gonna be ashamed to say it. I'm gonna say it in the interviews before and I'm gonna say it in the interviews afterwards. Jesus Christ healed me and if you don't believe it, I am sorry for you."

I made this point, "See, that is who God is looking for, people who will stand up for Him, people like you. In scripture He says, 'If you will deny Me before men, He will deny you before the Father.'"

"Steve, that's the whole thing in what I'm telling you. I would go in my room and pray to God and I would read the Bible and I would have all this faith, but then when I would go out before men I would be ashamed and shy. I'm not that anymore!'"

I roared with joy. Man, I'm telling you, Robert Brooks is a new man. God has healed him and called him to spread the good news of Jesus Christ. That a life surrendered to Him is a life that will be used. Robert gave me one last blast.

"I'm a new person. And I don't care who you are. When you come to my house, you'll talk about God, you'll see godly people, you'll see a cross around my neck, and I don't care, I don't care. I don't care if you judge me!"

Derrick Mayes had stopped over. He and Robert were going to chase the golf ball around for a while. I said my goodbyes.

What I learned that day is that Mr. Brooks wants you to know that you don't have to be a professional football player to receive a miracle. Your miracle is only a leap of faith away. The pool of living water in Jesus Christ runs deep. Robert Brooks spent the day with me praising Jesus because he missed the Super Bowl to learn what he has asked me to share with you now. Claim your miracle in Christ; it's done already.

The day after I met with Robert, this chapter was finished and off to the publisher. Then, a week later, I received a call that blew me away. It was from a lady by the name of Laura. She told me she had inoperable brain cancer, but when she was on a flight with someone she knew was a Packer, she felt an incredible amount of hope as she stood in his presence getting his autograph. Who do you suppose it was? You guessed it—Robert Brooks. This is just what Brooks had said the Lord had revealed to him, what would happen with others through His miracle.

She went on to tell me she miraculously came upon my book shortly after her diagnosis, and after reading it has had renewed hope as well. Yeah, I know it's getting wild, but I know this is just the beginning. Be forewarned—Robert Brooks is on a Holy Spirit rampage. He will be used in a huge way, again this season. Be assured of it.

On the day Robert checked into training camp, he asked me to drop off a copy of this chapter for him. I also brought him a photo of the two of us, me pointing to his "born-again" knee. I'd also picked him up a copy of Oswald Chambers' *My Utmost for His Highest*, a daily devotional, to help him put on some spiritual armor. As I drove away, I couldn't help but feel the anointing of our ministry we have and will continue to share.

Until recently, did you wonder, as I did, whether Robert Brooks would ever play football again? God told Robert Brooks he *will* rise and "jump" again into the seats at Lambeau Field and into the hearts of the people. He feels that God has promised it. And by the time you read this, it's probably happened.

As I watched Edgar Bennett lying on the turf during the Miami pre-season opener on July 26, 1997, I knew something wasn't right. At halftime Ron Wolf told Bill Jartz the bad news. Bennett had ruptured his Achilles tendon and was lost for the season.

I couldn't help but think about the possibility of one more miracle. All we have to do is get Robert to see him as soon as possible, I thought. Sure enough, as Brooks appeared with John Maino on the "Sports Extra" show the following day, Brooks said, "I dropped by Edgar's place and I told him, " 'It's gonna be all right, just keep everything positive.' "

As the show ended, Maino congratulated Robert on his incredible hard work in recovering from his knee injury. "Glory to God!" said Brooks, pointing upward. "It's God."

Will God do it one more time, this time through Edgar Bennett? Stay tuned, but in the meantime, remember that it's your prayers that make the miracle happen, and another miracle is just a leap of faith away. Just ask Robert Brooks.

Chapter 6

Love Always Works

It's patient and kind. It looks to build instead of tear down. It looks to give instead of take. It does not discriminate. It doesn't hold grudges. It gives second chances. And there is plenty of it around the Green Bay Packers. It's called love—and it always works.

It's hard to imagine the bond between fans and the team in Green Bay growing deeper, but even over the last year it has. Nobody says it's always been easy. But true love perseveres.

For more years than many of us diehard Packer fans want to remember, we woke up Monday mornings with a heartache. And for some, maybe even a headache. Our team had lost again. But a unique love, one that still survives today, helps to burn through the deep two-day mourning period. It's a kind of love that borders on insanity. By Wednesday after the game, it brings a sweeping wind of revival.

"Who are we playing Sunday," it will ask.

"The team that has won the last sixteen Super Bowls!" it answers.

"I don't care . . . we're gonna kill 'em!" we roar.

Is this you? Join the club. It's an attitude that surfaces from the depths of the Packermania virus. Greta Van Susteran, from CNN, who gave a cover endorsement for *Leap of Faith: God Must Be A Packer Fan*, also contributed this quote that too many of us can relate to.

"Being a Packer fan is like a disease. It's terminal. It never leaves you."

Well, like a disease you can either get bitter or get better. And Packer fans have chosen to love rather than abandon. In the long run it has paid off. Mike Vandermouse, from *Packer Plus*, says this has been the case with Packer fans.

"The fact the team went through nearly three decades of consistent losing, and still had undying love and loyal support, is remarkable." As he continues to share his take on the greatest fans, he brings up a point that has come to pass all too often in other markets where roots of allegiance aren't as deep.

"It's common for fans to jump on a winning bandwagon, but for some reason, Green Bay fans have been determined to hitch their pony to the Packers, through thick or thin."

Larry McCarren, who played for the Packers from 1973 to 1984, confirms this assessment. It goes back a long time, he says. "Even when we were lousy, the fans came out to watch us. Not only at home, but everywhere we went to play, there was always a pocket of Packer fans yelling and screaming for us."

Where does love come from? Hal Locke of Wausaukee, a pretty northeastern Wisconsin community, reminds us, "One of the fruits of the Holy Spirit is love (Galatians 5:22-23). When we allow God to exhibit his love through us it has an effect on those around us."

Love always works. Packer fans have shown the kind which has led to the beloved players leaping into the stands. As Robert Brooks says in his CD single, "Jump," they do it to give the fans a hug.

Loving can be tough sometimes. It's easy to hail the guy who's on top, but to love a hero after he has fallen, well, that can be tough. And it's happened in Green Bay. They haven't all been angels. He who is without sin anywhere may cast the first stone. A few bad boys have ridden into town, and to be honest, it's been tough to accept them. But love always wins out. Ask Andre Rison.

Here was a guy whose girlfriend burned his house down a few years ago! If his girlfriend didn't like him, how could we like him, or how was he possibly going to come in and not disrupt the chemistry of this team?

Were you one who said, "What are the Packers doing? Why would they risk bringing someone like him in, even if he was talented? Was it worth it to win, but sacrifice morale and comeraderie?" As you recall, however, Andre Rison worked out well with the Packers. What happened? What were the Packers able to do to change this man?

Here's what took place. On November 19, 1996, Coach Mike Holmgren asked Rison to leave any "baggage" he may have brought with him at Austin Straubel Airport and focus only on the present situation.

Rison was so grateful for the opportunity the coach was giving him. "He gave me another life. Not many people believe not only in my skills, but in me. I could play football forever, so, that's all that's needed. He thanked me and I thank him every day."

Just what did the Packer coach tell him? "It doesn't matter where you come from and what's happened. That's all in the past. You're starting from scratch with me." Well that Christlike forgiveness was just what Rison needed to release him from having anything to prove. After that, he was able to relax and do his best to fit in and just help the team.

The players immediately bathed him in blessings and well wishes. Brett Favre went first.

"Andre, I want you to catch a lot of passes. I'm going to be looking for you. I hope you score a load of touchdowns."

The receivers were next. Antonio Freeman, Don Beebe, and the others on the end of Favre's bullets also expressed their desire for him to succeed and know what it feels like to do the "Lambeau Leap."

The outreach for Rison, in this case, wasn't limited to the field. One of the first people to talk with Andre was Packer defensive lineman Sean Jones, who asked Andre over to his house for Jones' traditional Thanksgiving dinner.

The fans had the opportunity to put the squeeze on Rison after his very first touchdown pass at Lambeau Field. It may have come as a surprise to some that his stop in Green Bay never even brought a threat of crisis.

After the season, the Packers made a business decision to release Rison. Believing that he needed to be a starter, they let him go, knowing Brooks would be back in 1997. Could the love that kept him here survive the announcement the Packers were releasing him?

"I'm not disappointed. I'm hurt, but by no means am I upset with the Packers. This is a first-class organization. I thank them for the opportunity they gave me to get my career together, become a world champion, and show society I'm not what they think I am," he said gratefully.

Ron Wolf said, "The organization is indebted to Andre Rison. Speaking for myself and everyone in the Packers organization, we wish nothing but the best for Andre Rison."

Andre Rison reciprocated. "I'll remember everything," he said. "I met a lot of nice people, made new friends and new relationships that will last forever."

It's a fact that problems and controversy followed this young man like a rain cloud everywhere he went. What was it that was different in Green Bay? Did Rison change? Possibly. Did the people in Green Bay change? I doubt it. It appears that the great fans of Titletown were simply being themselves.

Pastor Mike DeLong says it really wasn't that surprising for Rison to have fit in as well as he did. He has his ideas as to why Andre was tamed in Green Bay.

"People are motivated to change and adapt when those around them are purpose-driven and vision-centered. When someone with authority speaks, like Reggie White, others (whether or not they know it is God speaking through that person) respond to them and desire to join them." Sounds like he maybe found a role model or two here.

"Great leaders inspire great followers to accomplish great things. Coach Holmgren is such a leader. White is such a follower and leader," Pastor DeLong added

Upon the arrival of this sometimes insecure, troubled man, the players and fans, along with Coach Holmgren, offered acceptance and forgiveness. To this man who fought to find meaning, he found a place, and most of all, he found love. He was showered with it in Green Bay.

Pastor Steve Petry agrees. "The influence of the believers on the Packers and the fans creates a loving family atmosphere where the 'one anothers' of the New Testament are put into practice."

The quickest way to a man's heart may be through his stomach, but it's not the only way. One of the most underhanded tricks a woman can play on a man is to cry to get what she wants. And we're sure glad one such trick worked in February of 1997.

Gilbert Brown had called a press conference to announce he had signed to continue his career in Green Bay with the Packers. Was it all about money? In this case, no. The man who has a sandwich (the Gilbert Burger) named after him explained.

Brown was doing an autograph show when a little girl approached him. As the girl drew nearer, the standout nose tackle detected something that caused him to stop dead in his tracks.

The young girl had a tear in her eye. When she spoke, she asked for something more than an autograph. She issued a plea, one that spoke louder than any words could have. It was as clear as the tear which glimmered in her eye.

"Don't leave," she pleaded sadly.

Brown was taken aback.

"I thought she was playing," he said. "But then I saw a tear in her eye and I was like, 'Whoa, this is serious.'"

That afternoon Brown signed a contract to play some more football in Green Bay. In his heart he knew that outpouring of affection was something he may never have received anywhere else.

Love. It takes the weapons out of enemy hands. It thaws when everything else freezes. It's indefensible. It makes bad boys good and big boys stay put. That's right, love always works. Just ask Andre Rison and Gilbert Brown. It's a shame that only one is back to feel some more of it.

Chapter 7

Packerwomania:
The Girls are Crazy!

PACKERWOMANIAC (Pak-er-wo-main-ee-ak) 1. A woman hopelessly addicted to the Green Bay Packers. Caused by an offshoot of the Packermania virus. A primary symptom is neglect of the victim's spouse during the Packer season.

There's nacho cheese all over her ruby-red lips. She violently smashes jalepeno-laced taco chips between them. Crumbs fall on her #89 jersey which she hasn't washed since "Chewy" signed it four years ago. Her blue eyes are focused on one thing—the green and gold-clad bodies on the TV screen three feet in front of her.

The Packers are taking on the Dallas Cowboys. It's just about over. The Packers lead by four touchdowns, yet she is still transfixed, her eyes glued to the screen.

Her husband walks into the woman's den. He has just come home from his weekly Sunday afternoon visit to the mall. This is how he copes with his wife's temporary insanity and insatiable Packer appetite. As if walking on egg shells, he sneaks up behind her green and gold recliner.

"Honey, are you still watching the Packers?" he asks dejectedly. There's no answer. He tries again. Maybe she couldn't hear because of the silver dollar-sized Packer helmet earrings covering her eardrums. He raises the volume of his voice.

"Sweetheart, can't we ever watch anything else on Sunday afternoons besides . . ."

"Can you hang on a minute?" she interrupts. "The two minute warning is coming up and you can talk then! Hold your horses, *pull-leese!*"

The lack of attention from this pickled pigskin-brained woman along with her words suddenly becomes a little to much for him to bear. He plops down on the couch, slaps his hands over his face and begins to cry like a baby.

"I don't know how much more of this I can take," he sobs. "Can we talk about this? Something needs to change."

After five seconds she retorts, "Yeah—OK—I might have some time after the post-game show with all the interviews and stuff—but I can't promise anything."

Like an addict lusting for more of her fix, she hungrily ingests more of what she yearns for—Green Bay Packer football. She can't get enough of it. After this game she will watch tapes of Packer games from last season. In many cases this leaves husbands to care for the kids, make meals, do the dishes and other housework.

Guys, does this sound like your story? Are the details so frighteningly real that it replays many of your horrific Sunday afternoons? I want you to know that you are not alone. I, too, live with a *Packerwomaniac*, a female addicted to the Green Bay Packers.

It takes one to know one and I can tell you there isn't any doubt that my wife suffers from a serious case of Packerwomania. She became a Packerwomaniac a few years after I rescued her from the cornfields of Clarion, Iowa, back in 1983. Here's what I have listened to since the Packers won the Super Bowl. "Can I get the latest Super Bowl sweatshirt? Can I get the latest Packer this-or-that?" I used to be the one who went a little overboard, but today the shoe has changed feet.

On opening day of the *Leap of Faith: God Must Be A Packer Fan* book tour, my wife was causing a commotion in Tampa. Green Bay had just dumped the Buccaneers. My mom, Aunt Joyce, and I are walking down the ramp in Tampa Bay's Sombrero Stadium. Suddenly

Top picture: Two of the cutest Packerwomaniacs in the country. McKenzie and Kayleigh Byrne, from Glendale, Arizona. They are three and five years old. Bottom picture: Two of the tiniest Packerwomaniacs, Lauren and Jordan Dalhoe, year-old twin sisters from Neenah, Wisconsin.

we hear this loud roar down below us where there was a crowd of Packer fans.

"What's going on?" I asked the ladies. As we rounded the next corner we saw Kim whirling her Packer towel over her head from high above the folks. They were reacting to her fanatical behavior. I was so embarrassed! I don't think she cared.

Is there a source of in-patient—or out-patient—help for these people? I'd like to tell you there is—but I can't. No one knows of any! It doesn't appear to be anywhere in sight, either. Learning how to tolerate it seems to be the best advice we can give you. That's right, learn to live with it. It seems to be permanent and irreversible. Keep in mind, God loves Packer fans, just like your wife, girlfriend, mother, or sister. Divine intervention may be your only hope.

One must ask, "Was it always like this? Even during the Lombardi Glory Years? Or do we have the guys on the current team to blame?" Whatever is the case, to those of us who live with a Packerwomaniac, it seems to be a permanent syndrome. Like Nestle's Quick stirred into a glass of milk, Packerwomaniacs appear to be inseparable from the Packers. The cases are widespread.

Donna Morgan, from Delafield, Wisconsin, is a classic example of one who suffers from the Packerwomania virus which has made her a Packerwomaniac. She is the victim. But the one who suffers is her husband, Bob. During Packer games he usually goes for walks in the park looking for lost puppies. For some reason, Donna is proud of her Packerwomania. She told us about some of the strange things it makes her do.

"I talk to the TV. On third-down situations I get real close to it. It's imperative that I record the games so I can go back and watch them again, later. I like to 'instant replay' the whole season! I really don't like to go to games much 'cause I like to be home to watch the slow-motion replays, so I can 'make the call'," she acknowledges.

While some die-hard Packer fans may have lost hope a few years ago, Donna and a couple of her friends never have. "During our losing drought, sometimes the only ones I could get to watch some games with me were my two dogs—Bandit and Lady. I trust the scripture where God says, 'Where two or three are gathered together in His name, the Lord will be there.' And God knows we and the Packers need His help!" In the end, really, all that matters to Donna is one thing. It helps to bring things into perspective.

"God is good. I believe He loves the Packers because they love Him. The most important thing is that God loves Packer fans— including me."

Deep in the heart of Wichita Falls, Texas, you can find another Packerwomaniac. Meet Chris Jung, a gentle Englishwoman. She had no clue what American football was, not to mention who the Packers were, until a couple years ago. That was when her husband, Bill, brought her to the U.S. from England. Her change began then.

In her sweet British accent she remembers, "I couldn't figure out why they called it football, when they were holding it all the time. Why do they keep hiding the ball? How can they see with those helmets on?"

Today, this gal's knowledge of the game would put most proud men to shame. "Somewhere along the line, I've discovered what it's all about, and it has clicked! Eureka! It's all fallen into place! I don't know how, but it all makes sense. I know there are some very complicated 'audibles' and miscellaneous things I don't pretend to understand."

Show me five of ten guys who know what an audible is and I'll give you a brand new 1997 Mercury Sable windshield wiper." She is definitely a Packerwomaniac.

With Vince Lombardi looking down from his place on the mantle, she says, "Woe betide anyone who talks to me just as Brett's about to throw the ball. I can't sit still. When we're close to touchdowns, I cover my face while peeking through my fingers while gripping Jesus' cross on my chain." Other than that, Chris Jung appears to be normal.

Last October, shortly after *Leap of Faith: God Must Be A Packer Fan* was released, Christine Winkelman, from Pewaukee, Wisconsin, called me about coming to speak to her youth group. I just about flipped when I heard her message on her answering machine. It was a singing message all about the Packers!

"Some nights during the season I would come home and the light on the answering machine would be flashing ten times," she told me. "No messages, just people wanting to hear my message tape." Her Packerwomania goes way back.

"I was certain from the time I was a little girl, my destination in life was to become one of the greatest Packer Backers of all time."

Her grandfather actually played against Curly Lambeau. "Guess who won," she says.

At the Winkelmans' there is a Green Bay Packer committee. In most homes, the man would head the committee. Not here.

"I am the president. Rule Number One is—official Packer gear is to be worn during games. And Two, everyone must answer the phone, 'Packer Hotline!'"

After I met Christine at a book signing and spent time with her after I spoke at her church, it became apparent that she is a bundle of energy and light for the Lord. She also sees God using the team for His glory.

"I love the team for their athletic ability, but more important, I respect them for their spiritual role as models for our youth. I enjoyed reading about them. Steve Rose used God as his quarterback and scored many touchdowns with many people," she says.

Our next subject is Judy Smith. This farmer's wife from Mukwonago, Wisconsin, also has a Jekyll-and-Hyde personality change about September 1. She waves her Packer pom-pons and winter neck scarf during the games. You can have your arm broken if you use a towel colored other than green during the season. Judy, tell us what happens in your living room on a Sunday during the season.

"A supply of green and gold jelly bellies and M&Ms are ready to be shaken after touchdowns. After scores, the kids and I eat three of each color for a field goal, six for a touchdown, and one for an extra point," she points out. Hmmm . . . what would that mean for a safety?

Judy and her son, Jesse, age ten, traveled to Green Bay without tickets for the NFC Championship game with Carolina. They sat outside in the cold in the their truck in the parking lot. They watched the game on a four inch screen! Between five long, cold walks to the porta potty, they did some screaming.

"We jumped out of the truck and yelled right along with the others. After the game we were jumping up and down and hugging everybody. What a celebration!"

Mysteriously, Santa brings a lot of green and gold for Christmas. And isn't it weird that the Packer stuff for Judy's husband, Paul, usually doesn't fit him?

"Someone has to wear it," says Judy, "so I make room in my dresser for it." Wow, what a girl! What a Packerwomaniac!

After hearing these cases, are you wondering if maybe you live with a Packerwomaniac? Here are a few signs and indications that you may be living with someone with this affliction.

10 Key Symptoms of Packerwomania and Signs You May Know a Packerwomaniac

1. On opening day of the NFL season, she says to her husband and family things like, "If you have anything to say, say it now, otherwise it will have to wait until after the Super Bowl!"
2. She feels that the weekly grocery money is much better spent on Packer merchandise and tickets, and fails to see why that might be a problem.
3. Before Packer games, she turns down the answering machine, pulls the shades, and locks the door. She also puts a sign on the television saying, "Anyone walking in front of this TV during the game will be shot!"
4. She totally abandons her "normal" Sunday routine for her "normal" Packer season routine.
5. She freezes with a glazed look on her face every time they show Mark Chmura's face during the game.
6. She is wearing two or more of the following at all times.
   A. green or gold eye shadow
   B. Packer earrings
   C. green and gold nail polish
   D. Packer sweatshirt, T-shirt, socks, sweat pants, stocking cap, helmet, slippers, visor cap, bathrobe, letter jacket, snowmobile suit, or evening gown (any or all).
7. She never swears . . . except after Packer interceptions and fumbles.
8. She hugs Brett Favre's picture every night before she goes to sleep.
9. She sobs uncontrollably, wearing nothing but black, for three days after a Packer loss. (She usually dries up by Wednesday.)
10. She has never heard of the Brewers, Badgers, or Bucks, but when you say "Packers," there is an unmistakable look of euphoria on her face.

If you know a gal who exhibits at least three of these ten symptoms, she very well may be a Packerwomaniac. Like my wife, Kim.

She was standing next to me one day as I signed a copy of *Leap of Faith: God Must Be a Packer Fan* for a friend. I accidentally ran my green felt tip pen across the bottom of her white Packer T-shirt she was letting me wear.

"Oh, no! You *can't* get that out!" she cried in panic.

"What about hair spray? Peanut butter mixed with ice cubes?" It was something I quickly recalled from home ec, back at Campbellsport High School, or from my grandma, I'm not sure which. "There has to be something," I said hopefully.

I tried to soften her disappointment. Then all of a sudden her frown turned to a sly grin, then a full-blown smile. I knew what she was thinking. I knew what was going to happen.

"No, wait," I begged. "C'mon, don't . . . I think you can get it out, really!" But the die was cast.

"Walmart opens at nine tomorrow morning." she said. "I read where they have a few of the new Packer shirts there." I followed her like a puppy dog, pleading with her not to invest in still more Packermania ware. But it was hopeless. By the next day at noon she was donning some new apparel. Guess what colors?

Men, although it may seem that there is no hope for your loved one who suffers, remember that there is always help for you. Ask God to give you the compassion to love your Packerwomaniac. Love the person and hate the madness of it all. It's not always easy.

You will be happy to know that a special foundation has been set up to help spouses like you. Consult your local directory to locate support meetings in your area. The foundation is called F.A.P.H., which stands for the Foundation for the Abused Packerwomaniac Husband. Don't wait. It won't get any better. But F.A.P.H. will help you to learn how to cope with what seems to be a hopeless situation.

Again, God loves Packer fans, even your Packerwomaniac. Let *Him* change her—because God does know you can't!

Chapter 8

Cheeseheads in Seattle

People in Seattle reacted as if a space ship had landed. It looked as though they thought it was an invasion. In a way it was! Seventy Cheeseheads had just gotten off a boat in Seattle.

We marched up the ramp from the Puget Sound Express passenger ferry *Argosy*. It was a historic event. It marked the the first Packer fan tour ever to arrive at an NFL game from a sea-going vessel. Green and gold flashed in the sea of Packermania. We began our march to the Kingdome and I'm telling you, the people in Seattle really thought we were off our rockers!

It wasn't as though they hadn't been warned. The little Pacific Northwest town of Port Townsend, where we had stayed earlier in the week, welcomed us with open arms. The village went so far as to paint some of the fire hydrants green and gold just to make us feel at home.

Steve and Dorothy Erban, our hosts from Creative Charters, of Stillwater, Minnesota, and Jim Coursolle, President of WPKR Radio, in Oshkosh, had graciously invited Kim and me along on the four-day jaunt. With the popularity of *Leap of Faith: God Must Be A Packer Fan*, I'd been asked to do a couple signings on the trip.

Steve Rose and Green Bay Packer Hall of Fame board member Jim Cour-solle, with Steve's first book, Leap of Faith: God Must Be a Packer Fan, *at the Green Bay Packer Hall of Fame.*

We all congregated at 5:00 A.M. on Thursday, September 26, at Billy Mitchell Field in Milwaukee. I was pleasantly surprised to find that Tim Kelley, a fellow 1978 graduate of Campbellsport High School, was taking the trip too. He and his wife, Karen, were getting a break from their five precious munchkins—and the farm.

We left the home of the Brewers on a 6:30 A.M. flight which took us to O'Hare Airport in Chicago. At 8:40 we were in the air for Seattle. And by 10:50, Pacific time, we were on a bus to Port Townsend, enjoying breathtaking scenery

Upon arrival, we Packer faithful were disbursed to bed-and-breakfast inns all over town. Kim and I stayed at the Bishops Bed and Breakfast. It was a charming little place. The hosts couldn't do enough for us. They carried our bags to our room and made us feel comfortable right away. We knew this trip was going to be very enjoyable.

There was an early eye-opening indication that we were no longer in Packer country. The windows were wide open—with no screens.

Holy cow, no mosquitos! If you tried this back in Wisconsin, the "state bird" would swarm and swallow you like a Packer in the front row at Lambeau Field.

On Thursday night we got acquainted with the town, dining at The Surf. It was fun spotting others from the trip and showing a little Packer sign or word of unity. You could hear people yelling across streets, "Go Packers!" The natives, who were primarily dressed in the "grunge look," thought we were kinda goofy. Well, that was probably mutual.

The next morning, beautiful sunshine crept over the mountains as I set out to jog. I usually have a pretty good sense of direction and didn't find it necessary to memorize any landmarks. I really didn't think there was any way I could get lost in this small town.

Famous last words.

About two miles into the workout, I saw a group of city workers on a side street. They spotted my Packer hat.

"The Seahawks are boss!" one smiled sarcastically.

I could tell he was just having some fun with me. After all, they did have a little home-town advantage and thought it safe to give me a little grief. "Go Pack!" I said as I raised my fist and breezed past them.

I had climbed very gradually until I caught a real view of the water. As I plodded along I thought to myself, "It shouldn't be a problem finding my back to the Bishops. I'll just continue taking lefts until I recognize something." But the more I ran, the less confidence I heard in that little voice in my head.

After an hour and forty-five minutes of jogging, here was this nice lady on a bicycle leading me home like Lassie. Only Lassie knew how to come home by herself. The others laughed at me when they heard what had happened. I really wasn't too embarrassed. Kim will tell you, if you take me anywhere for a couple days, I'm bound to do something embarrassing. It wouldn't be the last on this trip, either.

After I showered, Kim and I walked the main street looking for groceries when we found a deli. Next to the checkout counter, the headline in *The Leader*, the region's newspaper, proclaimed, "Packer Fans are in Town." And it went on to give this warning:

"If you see someone around Port Townsend this weekend who's wearing a hat resembling a hunk of yellow cheese, don't be surprised."

The story went on to tell how many Packer fans find it easier to get a ticket for an away game than one in Green Bay. That's a fact.

"It probably would take twenty-five years to get a season ticket, if you're lucky," Steve Erban told the paper. The story also noted that the Packers are the only NFL team owned by average people. By the time we left town, I have my doubts if they thought we were average people.

After lunch, we donned our Packer shirts and headed for the long beach along the coast. Tim, Karen, Kim, and I walked about four miles before we turned around. We stopped for ice cream. The tide nearly squeezed us in by the time we got back.

Everyone was freshening up, around five o' clock, while I napped. Then Kim woke me to tell me something interesting. "The power is out all over town. They think it could be a couple hours before it's back." I didn't think it was a big deal, until she explained that maybe the restaurant wouldn't be able to serve us dinner without power. Now, that could be a problem. I'm kind of like a dog. If I'm not fed every couple hours, I get crabby.

Word traveled quickly that there was a Chinese place that cooked with gas; they needed no electricity. That quickly became the dining hot spot, and we soon found ourselves seated there, about to have dinner by romantic candlelight. We were just about ready to order some exotic cuisine when the lights came on!

"Should we leave?" said Karen.

"Naw, let's stay here and try this," said her husband, Tim.

It turned out to be great food.

After dinner, we moved on uptown to a casual night spot. The people there were very friendly. The Packer contingent migrated upstairs where there was a pool table and some chairs and tables to relax. Kim was intense in her pool game. It was a great opportunity to get to know many of the other people on the trip. As we looked down from the railing, Wayne Mausser, the sports director from WPKR, and I had a great conversation.

"I think if the Packers can bust out early, it'll be over," Wayne said. It was a fun night.

Day three in Seattle was really an experience. The Kelleys, and Bill and Becky Ringenoldus, joined Kim and me as the whole crew took a boat to Victoria, British Columbia. We went to Butchart Gardens.

When we went in, all you could see were flowers, flowers, and more flowers. It's a great place if you like flowers. I really do . . . sure. Then again, when I had the chicken pox over Christmas vacation as a little boy, I thought that was great too. It came to about fifty cents a minute to look at flowers. "Take me to the game," is what I found myself saying.

After looking at more flowers, we rode back into town on the bus. The green and gold hoard was unleashed on Victoria for a few hours. The buildings there are incredible! I think that one of the motels had rooms costing $750 a night!

Exhaused, Tim Kelley and I decided to take a little nap on a lawn in the city square. All around us were street musicians, playing for money. As we were being serenaded, Kelley and I awoke and I found my briefcase open and loaded with coins. The gals, who have a pretty warped sense of humor, had made it look as if passersby were contributing to my cause. With friends like these, you don't need enemies.

A little while later we made our way to a Wax Museum, where I set off an alarm when I went to touch something that said, "Don't touch."

"This alarm really isn't on," I told Kim, and as I reached out, the alarm went off. It scared the daylights out of me, and I thought Kim was gonna die of embarrassment. The Ringcnouldous and Kellcys fell over in laughter. You can't take me anywhere.

By nightfall, we were watching whales and dolphins cavorting in the water as the sun went down. An hour later, we were back on a bus to Port Townsend. Someone led Packer cheers.

"I can't believe you grabbed for that thing and set off the alarm," said my embarrassed wife. I just shrugged my shoulders.

We went to The Surf for a bite to eat, and then it was beddy-by time. "Tomorrow's the big game," I thought to myself before I dropped off into a deep sleep.

The next day started early as we were picked up at the Bishops to be taken to Port Angeles for the floating tailgate party across Puget Sound on the *Argosy*.

It was very foggy as our journey began. As we ate a bountiful breakfast, we enjoyed some music played by a country band. We posed for pictures on the boat. The most unique photo showed everyone standing in the bow of the boat It was a sea of green on gold against

Top picture: What a crew! The Packer "sailing tailgate party," decked out in green and gold, arrives in Seattle aboard the Argosy. *Bottom picture: Steve and Kim Rose enjoy a Packer victory in the Seattle Kingdome.*

the blue water. I signed some books, posed for more pictures, and just soaked up every bit of the experience.

After three hours, the captain said we were going to be entering the harbor within fifteen minutes. Through the thick fog, we were beginning to see the city. What a sight when we spotted the skyline of the gorgeous city of Seattle! The game plan was to walk from the dock to the Kingdome.

"Here, put these on," urged Jim Coursolle. He was handing out WPKR bumper stickers. People were putting them on their clothing, their purses, and other items.

As we began to come into port you could see that there were hundreds of people waiting with eager anticipation to see us dairy screamers. They were standing about sixty feet away up on top of the ramp that led to the sidewalk. Televison cameras were pointing our way. Word had gotten out that the Cheeseheads were coming.

By 12:30, the boat was docked and the crew attached the ramp. It was time.

"Go Pack, go! Go Pack, go!" roared the contingent.

You simply had to be there to appreciate the looks of pure amazement on the faces of the Seattle folks, as they witnessed the loyalty of these Packer fans. At the top of the steps off the ramp, the TV cameras began backpeddling and asking questions as the one-mile march to the Kingdome began. The people of Seattle literally parted like the Red Sea. They didn't quite know what to make of us.

A couple in our group had those cute Packer helmets that inflate with air. Others waved Packer towels. Kim and I just soaked up the experience.

I have to admit, if a group of Detroit Tiger fans docked on the shore of Lake Michigan and walked to County Stadium in Milwaukee for a Brewer game, I'd find that a little wild, myself.

"Who's gonna win today?" asked a TV reporter as he pointed a microphone in one of the faces of our group.

"It's not going to be close. The Packers will win big!"

I handed a copy of my book to one of the media people. He smiled. As we strolled confidently on the sidewalk, you could sense that the homefolk thought we Cheeseheads were downright nuts! How could anyone be this crazy for a team? Of course, they haven't been in Green Bay for the last twenty-nine years, either.

As we passed a McDonalds I saw a lady who apologized as I walked past her. Actually, she may have been trying to start a friendly argument.

"I'm a Dallas Cowboy fan," she said proudly.

"That's curable," I said softly. "You don't suffer from anything a Packer Super Bowl win won't cure. I still love you," I joked as I hugged her.

As we approached the huge presence of the Kingdome, it became obvious there were a lot more Packer fans there than Seahawk fans. Walking on the street I could hear the loud voices of a couple of men boldly proclaiming a message written on sandwich boards they carried on their shoulders.

"There is an upcoming judgment!" one warned. "Have you accepted Christ as Savior?" announced the other. I'm not sure how many in our group were paying any attention to the men. The message sounded awfully familiar to me. It rang of the one Reggie White had been proclaiming ever since he came to Green Bay. I thought it took a lot of guts to stand out in the middle of all those football fans and yell out their message as they were doing.

As we slid throught he turnstile we were quickly enveloped by the Kingdome. As we found our seats and sat down, I realized that this was the same place where Ken Griffey, Jr. has launched many a home run. This was the same place where over the years Jim Zorn and Dave Krieg had worked for the Seahawks.

My seat was next to Jim and Diane Coursolle. We were perched in the second deck, comfortably in the southwest corner. As we gazed around, we could see that about 25,000 of the 60,000 on hand were Packer fans! It looked like Lambeau Field West. Quite a deal.

Here we were, two thousand miles from Lambeau Field, and you really couldn't tell the difference. The Packer die-hards turned portions of the Seattle home field into a sea of Green Bay green, dotted liberally with yellow Cheeseheads.

There was a buzz during the warm-ups. One of the sidelights of the story was that Eugene Robinson had returned to where he'd spent so many great years with the Seahawks. This day, he was the starting safety for the Packers.

As Jim Coursolle was paging through his Gameday program we talked about a cause Jim and Diane are quite involved in, the Christian

Children's Fund. I was deeply moved as Jim shared with me how this organization was helping kids all over the world by urging people to invest as little as twenty-one dollars a month.

"Steve, look at this," pointed out Coursolle. It seemed Chris Havel from our own *Green Bay Press-Gazette* was quoted in the NFL Gameday program. He had used the expression "leap of faith" in a way where it sure seemed more than coincidental that he was referring to my book.

"Do you think he got that from my book?" I asked Jim.

"I wouldn't doubt it," he quipped.

Ten minutes later, the Packers received the opening kickoff. On the first play from scrimmage, my friend Robert Brooks was just about killed. Brett Favre threw him a suicide pass over the middle. As Robert turned to run—*bam!*—he got drilled in the face mask. That hit would have broken most men's necks. I'm serious. As he lay on the turf, with Pepper Burruss and the Packer medical staff around him, it occurred to me that I might want to stay away from the road games. Just four weeks earlier, I was in Tampa when he got laid out on a pass play.

"Man, you gotta stay away from the games," Brooks would later joke with me.

The crowd offered warm applause as Robert was carted off the field. He had suffered a concussion. He told me later he didn't know whether he was "on foot or horseback." He equated it to being knocked out in a boxing ring.

The Packers struck first, right in the end zone near us. The touchdown pass that was pulled in by Antonio Freeman would have landed in my lap if Brett would have put an extra twenty yards behind it. But both teams struggled early. The most exciting play of the game was when Reggie White intercepted a Rick Mirer pass and ran out of gas before he could score.

After the slow start, however, the Packers pulled away with little trouble. The final score was Packers 31, Seattle 10. It was the first win for the Packers in a dome since January 8, 1994, in Detroit in the NFC wild-card game. There's no question, we nearly outnumbered the Seattle fans, but one thing was for sure, we outcheered them.

"I've never seen anything like what we saw today," said Seahawk quarterback Rick Mirer. "It wasn't what I've ever seen or felt at home before. But that's a tribute to those people. It's amazing."

Maybe we can call it the home field disadvantage, huh?

Milwaukee mayor John Norquist is a mighty proud Cheesehead these days. (Photo courtesy of Neumann Photography.)

The Packers were impressed too. "This is incredible," said Reggie White. "We're from the other side of the country and people came here to support us."

Former Seahawk Eugene Robinson, who had intercepted a pass for the Packers, also gave the faithful a nod. "These Packer-backers are no joke. They have the craziest fan base I've ever seen."

We enjoyed a few more hours in Seattle before we were ready to collapse at the airport for our red-eye flight home. Our plane left at 1:15 in the morning. The next thing I remembered is hearing the pilot say, "We are making our final descent into Chicago O'Hare. Please put your seats in the upright position." Three hours had passed and it really felt like about fifteen minutes.

We grabbed our bags and were heading to the bus which would take us back to Milwaukee. I'll never forget Jim Coursolle's words as we walked out of the automatic doors. It was still dark. Everybody was a walking zombie. I mean we were dead, all except for Coursolle.

Here it was Monday morning in the windy city of Chicago where the Packers were to play the Bears on the following Sunday. Who could be thinking about that right now? Most of us, we're thinking about a soft bed. Not Jim.

He marched out of the airport into the cool blast of a September morning, with a suitcase in each hand. I thought this young lady was gonna die as he marched towards her and in his bold, authoritive voice, asked her this question.

"Excuse me, could you tell us the way to Soldier field?" (Soldier Field is where the Bears play.)

The look on her face was unforgettable. It was as though she was watching a load of Cheeseheads getting off a boat.

Chapter 9

Another Starr at Rawhide

It was back in 1965 when a God-ordained intersection of dreams brought John Gillespe and Packer Hall of Fame quarterback Bart Starr together. The clash of these two servants' visions produced the Rawhide Boys Ranch in New London, Wisconsin. For the benefit of those who may not have read *Leap of Faith: God Must Be A Packer Fan*, we'll reiterate the miraculous story of how Gillespie and Starr and their wives became partners.

The Rawhide Founder recalls the story as if it were yesterday. Here's a golden excerpt, almost verbatim from the first *Leap of Faith* book:

> God had laid on my wife Jan's and my heart to start a Ranch for delinquent boys. We heard that Bart and Cherry Starr had the same vision. Jan said to me, "Why don't you call Bart?"
>
> Gillespie laughed to himself. His wife didn't seem to understand. This was August of 1965. The Packers were champions. Bart was very popular.
>
> "Honey, getting in touch with the pope would be easier, plus he'll have an unlisted number."
>
> "How do you know?" Jan echoed confidently.
>
> "Trust me, I know."

Two weeks went by as John tried to get in touch with Starr through the back door. In the meantime, a piece of property came up for sale that John thought would be ideal for the ranch. There were offers on it, but the owner really wanted to see it become a boys ranch.

With his own leap of faith, Gillespe put down a few thousand dollars of borrowed money on the property. Keep in mind this was in 1965. If you made $150 a week, that was big bucks. We're talking a lot of money, and the young Gillespies were carrying a big college debt.

Mrs. Gillespie persistently provoked her husband to try to call Starr.

"Okay, I'll show you," said John. "Just watch—he'll have an unlisted number."

Gillespie called information and amazingly got Starr's home phone number.

"Jan, even if we do get hold of him, he'll probably be too busy to meet with us," said her husband.

She persisted and he finally called Starr.

John recalls a man answering who simply said, "Hello."

"Is this the Starr residence?"

The voice said, "Yes, it is."

Is Mr. Starr home?"

There is no Mr. Starr here, but Bart is," the man replied.

"That's who I want to talk to."

"You're speaking to him."

After nearly falling off his chair, contemplating how he was going to explain this to his wife, he nervously proceeded.

"My name is John Gillespie. My wife and I have a desire to start a boys ranch for delinquent teenagers. We heard that you and Cherry may have the same interest. Is that true?"

"Yes, it is," replied the star quarterback.

Boldly, John continued, "Is it possible for us to meet with you sometime to discuss this?"

"Sure."

"How would I make an appointment?"

"Well, first you have to ask for one."

"I'd like to make an appointment."

"Great! Do you want to come over right now?"

After getting directions from Bart, the Gillespies set out to visit the Starrs to discuss the intersecting of Godly visions.

They arrived at the Starrs' modest, three-bedroom ranch home. Bart met them at the door and led them into the kitchen, where Cherry was making supper.

"I won't make this long because I don't want to mess up your supper plans."

Cherry then threw this forward lateral of love at the Gillespies. "If you make it quick, you will mess up *our* plans, because you're having supper with us!"

Gillespie felt as if he would wake up from this dream at any time.

The four ate supper.

John Gillespie began a low key presentation with flip chart showing the location, structure of leadership, game plans, and other information about what they envisioned for the boys ranch.

With a grateful grin, Gillespie remembers, "After each page, Cherry would say, 'Bart, that's just what we want to do.'"

Halfway through the presentation, Bart put his hand in the middle of Gillespie's book, looked over to his wife, and said, "Cherry, please let's hear what this couple has to say before we tip our hand!"

By then John had a good idea that the Starrs would lend their support to this project.

When the presentation ended, Starr looked over to his wife for her quick nod of approval. Then he turned to the Gillespies and asked, "How can we help?"

Gillespie went on to explain that his strength was not in fund-raising and asked for Starr's help in putting the capital together.

And so now, thirty-two years later, the non-profit Rawhide program has become one of the leading youth rehabilitation programs in the U.S. with close to an 80 percent success rate. Staff from other facilities around the nation visit on a regular basis, and this year the reputation of the ranch has crossed international boundaries.

The Russian government recently flew four of their high school educational staff who work with delinquent teens to Rawhide for three weeks to learn how the ranch operates. In particular, they wanted to know how Christian principles are integrated into the educational program at Starr Academy, Rawhide's high school.

Rawhide is indeed a program that teaches by role modeling traditional Christian family values. For more than three decades the

Bart and Cherry Starr with Jan and John Gillespie (left to right). Together they founded Rawhide Boys Ranch in 1965.

Starrs and Gillespies have steadfastly offered their lives as examples of those values.

Over the years, literally hundreds of people have played a part in the success of this wonderful youth program, but a special word should be said about Jan Gillespie.

In the early days, when John was traveling daily to raise desperately needed initial funds, and no other staff could be afforded, Jan was managing eight to ten delinquent teenagers, cooking, cleaning, counseling, doing secretarial work, caring for a small herd of horses, talking to visitors, all while raising their two young sons. Since 1965 Jan has been foster mom to 350 court-placed boys, ten at a time, each staying for about a year. There have been many late-night talks with hurting young men, lots of confrontations with frustrated young men, but Jan has always been caring, compassionate, and totally in control. She is always ready to share the real answer to life—a personal relationship with the Lord. She knows that God will truly fill that empty ache the boys have when they first come to Rawhide.

The love and caring of great people have blessed the ranch and helped it to flourish over the years. In this chapter, we bring you one more miracle that we know will give you great hope that there are many folks willing to go all out to share the bounty God has granted them. Grab another box of Kleenex and dive into this tale of love— pure love.

It was in the early '80s as John Gillespe was sitting in his congested Rawhide office peeling through a pile of papers. His phone was ringing. He picked it up to hear his wife Jan's voice on the other end of the line. She had jingled him from the home they were living in on the ranch.

"John, there is a couple here from Crandon, Wisconsin, who would like to see the ranch," said Jan. "Can you come up to the dining room to meet them?"

"Could you bring them down to the office?" John asked. But without answering his question Jan said, "OK, well, we'll see you up here in a little while." John knew that the visitors must have been standing there with Jan, and that Jan wanted him to come to the house at once.

Having people drop in was a normal, almost daily occurrence. But this visit would prove to be enlightening, very enlightening.

It took just a few minutes for the busy Gillespe to make the one-block walk home. Curiously he made his way into the dining room. Expecting to find the answer to this mini-mystery, he soon found the reason why he was asked to come to meet them there. There were Jan and a few of the boys sitting on chairs along with a lady. They were sitting around a man who was lying on his back on the floor. He didn't see any great panic so he assumed the man must have been all right, but it certainly was a strange sight.

"Honey, this is Bill Woods and his wife, Eddie. Bill's back went out on him, driving down here from Crandon," informed Jan.

"Hi, John, do you mind if I just lie here and we visit for a while?"

"Sure, that's fine."

After fifteen or twenty minutes the man got up very gingerly. No matter how busy John may be, he loves to share with others the dream the Lord so greatly put together beginning in 1965. John gladly showed Bill and Eddie around the ranch over a period of two hours. Then the couple left.

Three months later, a letter arrived at Rawhide with a very special message. It was from Bill and Eddie Woods. As if it were yesterday, John recalls the soft and encouraging words that graced its pages.

WE ARE WATCHING THE PACKERS!
IF YOU DON'T KNOW US, PLEASE GO AWAY.
IF YOU ARE FRIENDS, COME IN QUIETLY—
HAVE A DRINK-AND DON'T BOTHER US!
                    THE MANAGEMENT

Bill and Eddie Woods. Great givers—great Packer fans.

Hi John,

Thank you for the tour of Rawhide. We were very impressed. We think the world of Bart Starr and we have heard him talking about Rawhide on television and that is what prompted our visit. It was our opinion that if Bart Starr was behind it, it had to be a quality program, and after our visit we know that it is.

We would like to make a donation to Rawhide, but we would like you to come to Crandon to see what we would like to donate.

Very Sincerely,
Bill Woods

With eager anticipation, John and Jan Gillespe found themselves on the road to Crandon, about two and a half hours north of the ranch. They arrived at the estate, which was eight miles south of Crandon on County Highway W. John will never forget the breathtaking scene.

"We were driving on this winding road lined with stately trees. We rounded a bend, and sitting on the top of a knoll was a gorgeous log home overlooking a fifteen-acre lake," he recalls.

They were met by Bill and Eddie. They were soon fed lunch while having a warm chat. Still, there was no indication or hint as to the gift that the Woods wanted to give to Rawhide. John and Jan were then given a tour of the beautiful log estate home that Bill had built.

"We were just in awe of the beauty of this place and the grounds. We walked down by the lake. It was there that Bill began to give an indication of what he had in mind," remembers Gillespe.

"We have ninety acres and this is a private lake which is stocked with small- and large-mouth bass. This is our retirement home. John and Jan, if you think you could use what we have here to help boys turn their lives around, then we would like to give it *all* to Rawhide," said Woods.

The property was valued at close to $400,000. Today, it is close to $500,000! They also indicated that they would like to set up a $200,000 trust fund and would like the interest to go to maintain the grounds or for running a program, whichever Rawhide preferred.

They deeded the property to Rawhide. Today it is used as an ecology training center for young men, where they learn to appreciate wildlife and forest ecology and how to keep lakes clean. They learn about the environment as they camp out on this heavily wooded estate.

"The location is perfect. It's just far enough away so that it's a fun trip for the boys, but not far enough to be a long haul," says John gratefully.

Where did the Woods go? Today they reside in a retirement community in Beaver Dam, Wisconsin.

What or who could compel anyone to give everything they have to one cause? Even more mysterious is what kind of love propels this kind of generosity? In this case, it's two men. One is Bart Starr, but he is not the one who influenced the Woods the most. The one who moved them to do it was the Lord, Jesus Christ. It was their desire to honor Him with the fruits of their life. The Woods made a major gift out of love. It was this same love that prompted God to give all of us eternal life by the gift of his Son, Jesus.

God loves Packer fans, especially cheerful givers like Bill and Eddie Woods. You see, they believe as it says in the book of Proverbs that it is possible to give and get more back. With a leap of faith they gave everything they had to keep a God-ordained dream alive at Rawhide.

Oh, by the way, are the Woods Packer fans?. Yes, but they call themselves Bart Starr fans first, and Packer fans second. During every

Kids learning about the outdoors, thanks to the benevolence of Bill and Eddie Woods.

Packer game, the Woods displayed this two-by-eight-foot sign in front of their home:

> WE ARE WATCHING THE PACKERS! IF YOU DON'T KNOW US, PLEASE GO AWAY. IF YOU ARE FRIENDS, COME IN QUIETLY—HAVE A DRINK—AND DON'T BOTHER US!
>
> —The Management

Of course they were being a bit facetious, but the Lord will not be when He says to the Woods at the judgment, "Come into my Heaven, my good and faithful servants." And this will not be based on what they have given, but on the fact that they accepted Christ as Lord and Savior. And they backed up their faith up with action.

God loves Packer fans like Bill and Eddie Woods. The world would be a much better place to pass through if there were more like them. I'm sure the young men from the Rawhide Boys Ranch feel the same way, too.

In June of this past year, John and Jan Gillespie guided me through the facilities at the Rawhide Boys Ranch. I got goosebumps as I looked on the walls at the pictures of the many national personalities and celebrities who have come to help out by making appearances and fund-raising. I tell you that the Gillespies are one extraordinary couple. They have lived a very fruitful life in sacrificing themselves to help others. I am thrilled to call them my friends.

Friend, if you want a treat, take a tour of this beautiful place. I know John and Jan would love to share with you a smile, hug, or hand-shake—and a guided tour of a vision—one that was fulfilled through the obedience of a Godly couple, and a man, a great man, who just happened to play quarterback for the Green Bay Packers, and his wonderful wife.

Chapter 10

The Pack is Giving Back

I sneaked up behind the burly flat-topped lineman as he sat on the bench. He was taking a breather during a Green Bay Packer basketball game. I playfully wrapped my arm around his sweaty neck.

"Hey, I didn't know they let you out of 'the home' to play in stuff like this," I told the lug of a guy.

"I *thought* I smelled you," he snapped back at me with a big grin. I had forgot what a quick sense of humor this guy has. He doesn't look like a wisecracker, but I knew better. I'd been drilled by him before during a couple radio shows.

This lovable goofball was Packer Adam Timmerman. He's a farm boy from Cherokee, Iowa, who's done pretty well for himself. We were both down on the floor in the La Crosse Arena where some of the Packers had traveled to play in a basketball game against some Minnesota Viking players.

"I heard them say you were here," he did say seriously.

I had been invited to do a book signing there. About four thousand Packer and Viking fans were in attendance.

Timmerman, Craig Newsome, Bernardo Harris, and a few other Packers had boldly trudged through a wicked snow storm on March

Adam Timmerman with wife Jana at a charitable event. Scott Joffe, from AdCetera Sports Marketing, is in the middle.

24 to entertain the fans. I'm sure they had other things they could have been doing.

By the end of the game Timmerman was donning a tuba and playing with the band! If someone would have told him two years ago, while he was playing for the Jack Rabbits of South Dakota State, that he'd be a Super Bowl champ, and in demand for appearances, he'd have fallen off his tractor.

Adam is just one of many Green Bay Packers who understand that maybe they *do* have an obligation to give back to the community, that they *do* have a unique opportunity to reach people, especially kids. In his case, he is responding admirably.

He is just one of the many Packers who are glad to give of their time to the community. Understand that, especially for a professional football player, time is money, and often it is easier to give money than to donate time to a good cause. We all do it. If you are challenged to donate time or money, don't you sometimes choose the latter?

I am always amazed to talk with Robert Brooks, or to his associates, to hear about all he is doing to bless others. Aaron Rebman, a fourth-grader at Wilder School in Green Bay, is just one person who has appreciated being on the receiving end of Brooks' benevolence.

Brooks chose to make himself available for the "Bring a Packer to School" contest sponsored by JCPenny Co. Inc., the NFL, and Starter, a retail sportswear company.

Aaron had been chosen from 2,221 entries, and the moment he had waited two months for had finally arrived. The boy, who selected Brooks as the Packer he wanted to bring to his school, said his favorite part of "the best day of my life" was just sitting next to the speedy wide receiver during his two-hour visit.

Brooks took the opportunity to share with the students how the Lord had miraculously brought him along with his devastated left knee which he had injured against the 49ers.

"The doctors told me I would be on crutches for eight weeks. Reggie rubbed some oil on my knee and prayed with me. Two weeks later, I threw the crutches away. God is awesome."

Pretty bold words, because spiritual messages are not welcomed in the public schools these days. But you see, Robert Brooks is proud to be a Christian. He realizes it's a shame that they have kicked prayer out of the schools and brought condoms in.

"Trust in the Lord, He will help and guide you," Brooks urged the kids. "There is a purpose for everything, even my injury. God can take your hurts and make something good come from them, if you'll let him."

I wish I had a nickel for every time on the *Leap of Faith* "Temporary Insanity" Book Tour someone asked me, "Did you bring Reggie with you?" First of all, Reggie only hangs with quality people, and second if you only had an idea how many invitations Reggie gets. Debbie, one of Reggie and Sara's assistants, has told me more than once that Reggie gets five gallon pails full of letters every day.

As a matter of fact, Debbie once asked me if I would be willing to take some of Reggie's overflow of invitations for church engagements. Reggie is already being booked well into 1999. Everybody wants him—and he wishes that he could go everywhere, but he simply can't. If we could clone forty-six copies of Reggie, there still wouldn't be enough of him to do all the things he'd like to do, and go to all the places he'd like to go.

I was speaking at a morning service in Wisconsin last April. I had talked about Reggie's big heart, and how he gives to the community here and in Tennessee. Afterwards in the narthex of the church, I was receiving some hugs and handshakes and signing some books, when someone slipped this note into my pocket and walked away. It read.

> Mr. Rose,
>   I loved your message about our Lord and Savior, Jesus Christ, the Packers, and your life. But, when you mentioned Reggie White and how he is with the people, and how he treats them, I looked over at my son. He looked upset and started to lose interest in what you were saying.
>   I asked him, "What's wrong?"
>   He answered, "If Reggie White is such a good person and his fans mean a lot to him, and he knows the Golden Rule, I don't understand why he hasn't answered my three letters."
>   Steve, if you see Reggie, tell him to remember his fans as he remembers the Lord. My son sent Reggie his own wrestling sports card, and I feel Reggie should go by the Golden Rule.
> Dan

Dan and all Christians, let me tell you how much I know Reggie White would love to answer personally all of his mail and phone calls. But you just can't imagine just how much in demand and how much mail and how many phone calls Reggie and the others get every day. There are other boys and girls who aren't getting their letters and calls answered either, and trust me, Reggie wishes he could, but he just can't. There are just too many requests. I hope this helps you to better understand and I hope that, as Christians, you can forgive Reggie.

The spotlight can be not only overwhelming for the Reggie Whites and other superstars, but scary, too. Dig this. Brett Favre is famous enough to be walking down a street in St. Louis, be recognized by a group of fans, and literally chased into the safety of the team's hotel. Yet Favre is normal enough to be serving hot dogs to the kids at a Green Bay school a couple of days later. Nobody would blame any of them, including Favre, if they stayed home and avoided everybody. But he won't do that. He's giving back.

Way too many times we hear bellyaching about the money that the players make. But no one is quicker to give than Brett Favre. Scott

Joffe, president of AdCetera Sports Marketing, knows first hand. He regularly works with Favre.

"Many times I have heard of a special cause that I know Brett would like to be a part of," remarked Joffe. "I have sent footballs to him to be autographed and he has overnighted them back."

Last Winter, Brett gave away 4,444 (his number is 4) autographed jerseys during stops at the Children's Hospital and the Boys and Girls Clubs of Milwaukee. Last season, nearly $250,000 was distributed by the NFL MVP quarterback through the Brett Favre Foundation.

Craig Hentrich gets *his* kicks by giving of himself. In March, the Packer punter, along with defensive tackle Bob Kuberski and public relations director Lee Remmel, helped to raise more than $22,000 for Prevent Blindness Northeast Wisconsin at the 1997 Celebrity Luau.

Picture these guys dressed as if they were from Oahu, Hawaii! By teaming up, they helped to raise funds by acting as waiters to more than four hundred guests at the Watering Hole, in Green Bay. Thanks to their unselfishness, thousands of children and adults can receive free eye-health programs and vision-screening services.

At the start of last season, two of the Packer players were given awards as "Unsung Heroes." The honor is given to NFL players for accomplishments—on and off the field.

A member of the NFC's 1996 Pro Bowl squad, Mark Chmura is the Packers' Untied Way representative, in addition to being involved locally with Children's Hospital of Wisconsin and Big Brothers/ Big Sisters.

Eugene Robinson, who was heavily involved in community work in Seattle, is a frequent visitor to hospitals.

How would you like to have a couple of Packers show up in your backyard to play a little "pickup" game? Well, that's just what happened to Taryn Stewart. In June, Mark Chmura and Adam Timmerman traveled to Taryn's Sheboygan home for a game. She was the lucky winner in Shopko's "Play Football" contest.

For the game, Chmura was listed at 6'5", 250. Timmerman 6'4", 295. Taryn is listed at 4'7", 70. She's about the size of the heart of a bunch of these unselfish guys, the ones who wear green and gold on Sundays, doing whatever they can to give back—even if it means showing up in somebody's backyard for a little football game.

The scene switches to Children's Hospital. A slightly-built Packer walks into a room where a little boy is having a tough day. He's very sick and has chosen to be an introvert and not talk, not smile. There was even a bigger problem. The boy was a Cowboy fan.

"Hey, pal, you can smile, can't you?" asked the man.

The boy sat motionless. The player mockingly went to take some of the boy's potato chips. Sticking out his hand to block the player's reach, the boy almost smiled. Very soon, the boy was sharing his chips and jello with his new friend who had worn him down with his warmth and love. The boy was smiling.

"I have to go," said the Packer. Now the boy was glum with the news of his new friend's parting. "Here, let me sign this for you." It was the front cover of a *Sports Illustrated*. And with that—one Desmond Howard flashed yet one more Super Bowl MVP smile and then walked out of the room.

There was a smile equally as big on one young former Cowboy fan.

Chapter 11

A Night in Wisconsin

When in Rome, do as the Romans. When in Wisconsin, do as the Wisconsinites do. That was, and continues to be, the motto for a couple down-to-earth guys who arrived in Green Bay from the "left coast." Ken Ruettgers has enjoyed a lot of special Friday-night cuisine in the twelve years he has been here. He decided to share this cultural experience with a friend.

Ken Ruettgers and John Michels have a lot in common. Both are from California, both went to USC, both were first round draft picks, and they have a slew of other commonalities. It's really pretty spooky.

In April of 1996, Michels found himself, as Ruettgers had eleven years before, a rookie on the Packers. Even though John had been picked to take Ken's position, Ruettgers took Michels under his wing. Over the last two years he has done what he can to introduce John to the good life. Michels is happy he did.

Both of these guys know the feeling of being trapped in the smog-filled fast lane of southern California. And a year and a half after Michels' arrival, Ken thought it was about time for a fellow Californian to experience the peace, pride, and a real joy of Wisconsin—some Friday night fish!

Even to natives of Wisconsin, the "Friday Fish Fry" thing is kind of a mystery. When and how did it start? Speculation says that the heavy Catholic population in Wisconsin may have something to do with it. On Fridays, they gave up meat in favor of fish.

It really makes no difference where this great tradition came from. If you have never jammed some fresh lake perch into your craw, or tasted the sweet walleye pike that can be found in these parts, you don't know what you're missing.

In the early evening on a Friday night in spring, John Michels and his new wife Melissa, and the Ruettgers' family, Ken, Sheryl, and the kids, set out to experience this popular Wisconsin dining ritual.

"Ken had always told me about Friday night fish fries in Wisconsin," said John. "I told him, 'You know, I've never done one of those yet.'"

"You're kidding," the elder, now retired lineman said somewhat astoundedly. "You don't know what you're missing. We have to take you out for one. You need to enjoy 'A Night in Wisconsin!'"

How much of a cultural experience was it for the Michels?

"On the drive down it was just like I pictured Wisconsin to be. We saw barns out in the middle of nowhere and cows in the field." His view was from Ken Ruettgers' white Chevy Suburban as it headed south from Green Bay towards Kaukauna.

Within thirty minutes of leaving town, they were at Van Abels Supper Club in Hollandtown.

"The place was packed. Luckily, Ken had reservations, so we were able to get in. After a couple soft drinks they took us to our table," remembers Michels.

Not only was this a treat for the Michels and Ruettgers, but for the folks who just happened to be in the same place as these behemoths and their petite wives.

"Ken, thanks for all you have done," remarked one supper club patron.

Another approached with his grandson. "Thanks for bringing the title back to Titletown, you guys."

"The people here are so nice and friendly," says Michels fondly.

Have you ever watched one of those movies or soap operas where one guy orders on behalf of everybody and the table? Well, that's not quite what Ken Ruettgers did, but it was close.

Top picture: Ken Ruettgers and family enjoy an outing. Bottom picture: The handsome John Michels, co-host with Steve Rose of the "Timeout" show, and his lovely wife Melissa. The Michels were married in February of 1997.

As he held his menu, he looked at those with him. "Now, you guys, this is gonna be 'A Night in Wisconsin.' We have to keep that theme, OK?" Everyone agreed.

A star-struck waitress took the orders for mounds of walleye pike. Packer potatoes, which are hash browns pasted together with gooey Wisconsin cheese, were a natural. (Legend has it that one of the Packers of the Glory Days ate them often.)

As chief spokesperson for the contingent, Ken added some necessary condiments to the multiple-course feast.

He looked to the waitress and added, "We'll also take a couple orders of cheese curds—and, oh—how about some milk?" he finished.

The ice cold, creamy milk washed down the succulent cheese curds while the fish fried in Van Abels' kitchen. Within twenty minutes, the gorge fest was on.

"We ate a lot of food—I mean a lot of it. I was just doing what coach said," Michaels laughed.

What was he talking about, following orders by eating everything in sight?

Now, John Michels is a nice young man. Packer public relations chief Lee Remmel told me he had never been as impressed as he was with Michels just after he was drafted. Especially the way he carried himself at his first press conference.

I can concur he's a great guy. Doing a few radio shows with him last year was a ball. He's transparent and real, no phony balony about him. I'm not out to create any jealously between any of us and him, but I really feel I must point out the following:

After the 1996 season, Coach Holmgren asked John Michels to put on some weight, to bulk up. That's right, put on some weight! I don't know about you, but to me that is downright disgusting. While we're slamming slender drinks and eating rabbit food till our ears are green, this guy is on a seafood diet. (He's told that, if he ever sees food—to eat it!)

I can testify that Ken has never had too much of a "food conscience," either. I recall in 1995 trying to convict Ruettgers on the air ("Timeout" show) of dunking crab legs in pools of butter, and of too many stops at the Dairy Queen. He'd point to his hips and say, "It's for my goal line muscle!"

A hour and a half later, Michels admitted he was about as happy as a fish in Lake Michigan. But he did have one thing in mind—dessert.

Ruettgers read his compadre's mind. "Later, we will finish off the evening with a tasty treat from here in the nation's dairyland. You'll all love it."

The check must have been quite impressive. Nobody was spotted doing the dishes, so we assume the liability got covered.

On the way out, the crew spotted something that they felt really could make this night perfect, something to complete their "Night in Wisconsin." There are a couple bowling alleys at Van Abels, and the senior member of this family thought it offered a perfect opportunity.

"How appropriate. You can't say you're from Wisconsin if you haven't bowled a few lines," said Ken. "The lanes weren't open, but the owner was nice enough to open up so we could have our family enjoy a couple gutter balls!"

It was somewhat humbling for Michels. Not just the score, but what occurred.

"Ken had just finished telling me how he once went a little too far down the alley, lost his footing, and fell on his back," said Michaels. "Within a couple throws, there I was, myself, down looking up." Like veteran, like rookie.

A few hours and a couple of pounds of pike later, the clan got back into the Ruettgers' Suburban. Gas mileage must have suffered some, one would assume, during the ride back to town.

Ken had promised one more treat. A half hour later they were pulling into a parking lot on Oneida Street, just down the road from Lambeau Field. As they looked up they saw a sign that said, STORHEIM'S CUSTARD. It was time for dessert.

"I had some chocolate custard and Ken had vanilla. It put a real exclamation point on quite a night," smiles Michels.

John Michels and Ken Ruettgers walking side by side may never look as if they fit in a land of diminutive folks in Wisconsin. But they want us to know they try to fit in wherever and whenever they can. They like it here.

If you see two giants eating up a heap of walleye pike anytime soon, ask if you can sit down and join them. They know how to do it up right. Hearing about this "escapade of the stars" reminds us homefolk that sometimes we forget how fortunate we are and take for granted the privilege we have of regularly enjoying "A Night in Wisconsin."

Chapter 12

Packers 101:
Heroes and Heroines

When was the last time your high school geometry class helped you pay a few bills? Have you looked heavenward recently and thanked God for knowing calculus? Those classes were, and still are, important in some circles. But there are courses that seem to be just a little more pertinent than others. Have you ever heard of "Packers 101: Heroes and Heroines?" It's a study of role modeling and you can thank God and a few of Packers for it.

I have to ask myself, "What if there had been such a course at Campbellsport Southwest High School when I was there?" Now I really could have used that. Maybe I would have learned how to treat people a little better than I did, and been a better example for others.

Where is "Packers 101: Heroes and Heroines" found? Is there really such a course anywhere? Yes! Influenced by a few of the teddy bears you've seen at Lambeau Field on Sunday afternoons, a teacher by the name of Mr. Donald Casey, Jr. has brought it into existence. He has watched the major influence that many of the angels in green and gold have had, both in past years and today.

One only need listen to any of the kids in two-time Super Bowl MVP Bart Starr's old Green Bay neighborhood to know how he blessed them way back during those "glory years." Or hearing the stories of how the gruff Vince Lombardi turned into jello when he was around kids. And it continues today without having skipped a beat.

So, most of us in Wisconsin know of the impact that many of the Packers of yesterday and today have had around Green Bay. However, we have much less knowledge of how the Packers are affecting the rest of the country. Recently, I heard of one example, from Monroe, Connecticut.

A few months after the Packers' Super Bowl win, I was making my way down the steps to the lower level of the Green Bay radio studios of WORQ. I had stopped at "Q-90" to pick up the tapes of the "Timeout" programs. I was using them for research for this book.

As I walked through the building, I thought of Packer memories, great memories. I thought of the late afternoon walking alongside Sheryl Ruettgers, my hand on her husband Ken's back, as we walked down these same stairs together.

It was back in August of 1995. Ken had broken four little bones in his back. He had a copy of his book, *Homefield Advantage: A Dad's Guide to the Power of Role Modeling*, in his hand. It had just come out. Little did he know the ripple effect it was going to have. In a few minutes I'd get another dose of Kenny's influence through his writing, which is brought to life through his living.

As I walked into Studio A at the WORQ studios, I saw Kid, the program director at the station. He had just returned from his honeymoon. "Kid, how you doing?" I asked. I shook his hand and grabbed a handful of his long black hair as I hugged him. "It takes about a year before it all starts to unravel, you know!"

"No, man, we're doing great, but thanks for the encouragement!" he laughed as he reached for another CD to throw in the deck. "Here are the tapes from last year for you. There's also a package that came here for you a couple of months ago," he added.

The tapes sat in a box that was folded shut. Next to it was the package. Little did I know what a treasure and blessing it would turn out to be. It would really reinforce and lend more evidence to what we know already. It is that many of the Packers have a tremendous influence, not only in Wisconsin, but all over the country. I leaned on the same counter where I had sat and learned this while doing the "Time-out" radio program since 1994. I grabbed the package.

On the front of it was printed,

PLEASE FORWARD THE ENCLOSED MATERIAL TO MR. STEVE ROSE, OF NEENAH, WISCONSIN. THANK YOU! THE SPECIAL EDUCATION CLASS OF DONALD CASEY, JR.

On the other side in the return address portion it read,

Donald Casey, Jr., MS
Professional Educator
Stepney Elementary School
180 Old Newtown Road
Monroe, Connecticut 06468

I was intrigued. Mail is always fun, but this package really had some pop to it. God was about to move on my heart in a very special way.

"Take care, my friend. I gotta go. Kim is in the car," I told Kid apologetically.

"Hey, keep in touch, bro," he replied.

"I will."

When I got into the car, I tossed the package into the back seat. Within minutes, my wife Kim and I were eating at the Backgammon Pub on Oneida Street.

"That's a package for me that someone sent back in February," I told her. "It's from Connecticut. I can't figure out how he found us."

"I wonder what's in it," she said.

After dinner I told Kim that I was going to go to the little boys room. When I came out I found that she had pulled my car up to the restaurant door for me. One of her favorite shows, "ER," was on at nine o'clock and she wanted to make sure she was going to get home in time to watch it. With the boss driving, I had a chance to end the suspense and open the package.

As we flowed down Highway 41, I reached into the back seat and grabbed it. I found a T-shirt, a tape, and a spiral binder. As I opened it I went from pretty serious to awfully weepy in about one minute and five seconds. On the letterhead from Stepney Elementary School in Monroe, Connecticut, was written this warm letter:

Mr. Steve Rose, Author
Leap of Faith

Dear Mr. Rose,
    My name is Donald M. Casey, Jr. I am an 11-year special education teacher at Stepney Elementary School located in Monroe, Connecticut. I have 30 children in my classes with special needs who are in grades first through fifth. My children are great and I really love them.
    Children today have few positive role models in their lives. In order to meet this need and in some cases provide children with positive role models, I have designed a CELEBRATION OF EXCELLENCE award-winning curriculum educational project entitled "Heralding Heroes and Heroines." Children study an individual who is a positive role model in his/her community. Using reference material, children research the individual's life, write a class book, and make a video. All of our work is shared with our chosen role model. Children invite their Hero/Heroine to school for a special day of recognition.
    I want to congratulate you for writing a wonderful book which I just finished reading. I was truly inspired and learning more about the Packers and how they serve as wonderful role models makes me even prouder to be a Packer fan.
    Most important, I learned more about Mr. Ken Ruettgers. This past fall of 1996, the children studied about Mr. Ruettgers as their "Class Hero & Role Model." We studied his book *Home-field Advantage* and did his "Halftime Pointer" called "Help A Child Find A Hero." We wore our Packer shirts, sang our "Hero" and "Packers Polka" songs, wrote letters, and researched Mr. Ruettgers' inspirational life.
    Enclosed please find our Mr. Ruettgers project for you to enjoy. You will find a cassette tape of us singing songs for Mr. Ruettgers on Side A. On Side B, please find a radio interview with former Packer Mr. Jeff Wilner.
    This spring of 1997, we will be studying Mr. Eugene Robinson.
    Thank you for your time, Mr. Rose. The children also want to present you with a Monroe, Connecticut, T-shirt. I loved your

book. My favorite photo is when Mr. Ruettgers turned his helmet
into a pumpkin against the Bears. When you see Mr. Ruettgers,
please tell him we wish him a healthy recovery from his knee
injury and God bless him and his family.

God bless you, Mr. Rose
Donald M. Casey, Jr.

As I read the portions about how they were using Kenny's testimony and example for their curriculum, I have to tell you, I wanted
to cry. There aren't many things that can bring me to tears, and very
few people, but the mention of Ken Ruettgers is one of them. You see,
for years I've told people that the greatest thing about him had nothing to do with football. Someone else way out in Monroe, Connecticut, has realized it too.

When I got back to our Neenah home I couldn't get to the phone
fast enough to give this special man from Connecticut a call. He had
also indicated that he has been a lifelong Packer fan and that he really
liked my book. Both of those comments revealed this was a very intelligent man! Really, I wanted to thank him for what he was doing for
his kids and compliment him on his choice to honor the guys, specifically former Packer Jeff Wilner and current Packer speedster Travis
Jervey. But I especially wanted to let him know what a great choice I
thought he had made to feature Ken as a positive role model for their
semester study.

It was about 9:30 P.M. our time and I knew it was about 10:30 on
the east coast, but I didn't care.

"Hello, is this Don?" I asked.

"Yes."

"Don, this is Steve Rose. How are you doing tonight?"

Before I could say another word he proclaimed, "What a great
book!"

"Don, that's not why I'm calling, but I really appreciate your kind
words. The reason for contacting you is to congratulate you on your
award-winning course in your school and to pass along my affirma-
tion on your choice to feature Ken."

Mr. Casey began to explain what he was doing. "I guess I've been
really impressed by the way that Mr. Ruettgers"—Casey calls almost
everyone Mr. or Mrs.—"has always talked about the importance of

his family," he said. "Mr. Rose, we have been so blessed to have the kids study Ken. Mr. Ruettgers was nice enough to write us a letter, too. We feel that it is so important to help the kids find role models."

Let me tell you, a chat with Donald Casey, Jr. will pump you up! If his enthusiasm could be bottled and sold there would be no singing of the blues, anywhere! He's a 35-year-old fountain of hope with an infectious optimism.

Obviously, Donald Casey has little room for cynicism. He sees a world with heroes—among them a few of the Green Bay Packers—and he wants his students to see them, too.

Casey told me he works as a special education teacher with kindergarten through fifth-grade students. Many of his pupils have speech impediments, social or emotional troubles, learning disabilities, or neurological impairments. There are certainly more glamorous opportunities in education, but that's not important to Don Casey.

The "Heroes and Heroines" class helps to improve the children's academic skills—reading, language, math, and research—as well as improving self-esteem, and it provides them with role models.

Even though they're elementary students, not only do I want them to look up to people, I want them to be role models themselves," Casey says. "I stress that they are role models."

What did Kenny Ruettgers think of being honored?

"It's incredible to know that you're having that kind of an effect on kids. It's an honor and a responsibility," said the retired lineman.

Packer safety Eugene Robinson was the Stepney Elementary School 1997 Class Hero. A proclamation to Robinson noted he was a native of Hartford, Connecticut. Another great choice, you guys.

As part of the "Packers 101," Ken Ruettgers' curriculum at the school, the children made up some fictitious math problems to hone their skills. I was really grabbed by problem No. 9 on the sheet. It was from a fourth grader.

> 9. Matthew, (Ken's son) had three scoops of ice cream. His father,
> Ken, ate one scoop of Matthew's ice cream. How many scoops
> are left?

Now, the obvious answer is two, right? Wrong. It's a trick question. As someone who has been drawn into an addiction to Ben &

Jerry's ice cream, thanks to Ken, and one who has been caught hangin' at the DQ with him, too, I can attest to this. The real answer is none!

You see, I am sure there's no way Ken would have eaten just one scoop. I'm sure he would have polished it off! But we know what you mean. Thanks for bringing this math problem to us.

Friends, I think there's more than one hero here. Along with Ken Ruettgers and Eugene Robinson, I would like to thank one more hero and role model. His name is Mr. Donald Casey, Jr. Thanks for introducing the Packer role models to your class, and to the world. We salute you, Don, for initiating "Packers 101: Heroes and Heroines." Its true impact may not be known until you, thou good and faithful servant, meet the Lord face to face.

If you are involved in education anywhere in the world, Don Casey would love to make a copy of his "Heralding Heroes and Heroines" teachers manual available to you. To order, simply send $25, plus $3 for shipping and handling, and include a 9x12-inch self-addressed envelope. Send it to Don Casey, Jr., Stepney Elementary School, 180 Old Newtown Road, Monroe, CT 06468.

Chapter 13

There's No Place Like Dallas!

It came as a bit of a surprise, but not a shock, to learn what a fun, warm place Dallas is! I mean that. We stopped there on the book tour. Being so far away from home it just didn't seem likely that those people would be so friendly to a stranger. The fact was, they were super! No, they were more than that. They were some of the most classy, loving people I have ever met in my whole life. I really mean that, and feel the need to acknowledge this truth. More folks around Green Bay could use some people relations lessons from the great people I would meet in Dallas in a few hours.

I had to wonder, with all the opportunities for speaking engagements around Green Bay, why I was going all the way to Dallas? Was I crazy? I think even I know the answer to that!

I'm not real fond of travel. However, the *Leap of Faith* "Temporary Insanity" Book Tour has had me sprawled all over the country since September of 1996. It's been a ball. We had been in Tampa, where we did a signing alongside Packer great Ray Nitschke. What a great guy! From there we went to Seattle. Later stops landed us in Louisville, Kentucky, and in the heart of Wisconsin for a good share of book signings.

Home for Kim and me is Neenah, Wisconsin. We love it there, but God hadn't called me to write *Leap of Faith: God Must Be A Packer Fan*, as well as this one, to keep these books a secret. Part of the responsibilities of ministry is going wherever you are called to go. Maybe Dallas wasn't Africa, but I wasn't sure how I would be treated there, so far away from home. But I like meeting new people, seeing new places, and trying to learn from others wherever they may be. But Lord, why would you be sending me to Dallas?

It was 6:30 A.M. on March 9, 1997. I stood in the doorway with a business suit in one hand and briefcase in the other. I closed my eyes and kissed Kim goodbye.

"I won't be home till late tonight. Not only are we in Dallas, but we have one other stop today on the circuit," I reminded her.

"I love you," she said as she hugged my neck.

"Love ya too." It's always right about here that I get the big lump in my throat, when I need to make a dash for the car because I don't want to let my wife know that I might not be able to talk. You know, she might realize that I miss her and that would make me pretty vulnerable, wouldn't it?

Two minutes later I was accelerating my blood-red Mercury Sable down Harrison Avenue in Neenah. I put a Charles Stanley album on the tape player. The sky was dark and blustery. It could have been nicer, but this was par for the course for this time of year in Wisconsin. It was hard to believe, but in four hours I would be in an Assembly of God Church in Dallas. It hardly seemed possible.

It never fails that I have huge butterflies in my stomach before I speak. The only thing that seems to bring a sense of peace in these situations is prayer. With my eyes open and on the road, I began to talk to the Lord.

"Heavenly Father, I pray that as I travel now you might deliver me safely to my destination. I pray that you would be the message today and allow me to just be the conduit for your words. So, God, prepare hearts for what you want me to do in Dallas today. And God, I hope the weather is better there than it's been here!" I prayerfully pleaded. I'm not sure how important the weather is where God is sending you.

Four hours later, at 10:35, I found myself in Dallas. I was still nervous. I had never been in Dallas before. John Peterson, the former

Olympic gold medalist on the U.S.A. wrestling team, lives near Dallas. He had told me some things about this part of the country. I wouldn't be disappointed.

One of my prayers was answered as I arrived. The weather was much better than it was at home. The distance I'd traveled in those hours thankfully had provided a temporary reprieve. It was absolutely gorgeous. The bright sunshine felt good as it penetrated the windows of my car. The rays glistened on the hood as I drove into the parking lot of the Assembly of God Church. I got out of the car.

"You must be Steve Rose," smiled a tall man as he shook my hand.

"I am, but don't hold that against me," I joked as I clutched his hand before shaking it. The butterflies had just been tamed a little, but not much. Soon, there were others surrounding me. These folks were no different than the thousands of others throughout the country who were coming out to find out just why "God Must Be A Packer Fan."

"Do you need some help with anything?" asked a young man of about sixteen.

"Oh, it would be so kind of you to carry these two boxes for me," I replied very gratefully, standing next to my open car trunk. They contained books and the many poster-size pictures of me with some of the guys on the Packers. I was curious to see how the young Dallas gentlemen would react when he caught a glimpse of Reggie, Brooks, Ruettgers, and me.

"Wow, those are some pretty big guys, huh?"

"Yeah, can you tell which one is me?"

I always ask because so many people confuse me with Ken Ruettgers. I always have to tell them that I'm the one wearing glasses!

Seconds later we walked up an entrance ramp that was used for wheelchair access. I noticed people coming in at a nice clip through the main door. That's why we chose the strategic entry that we did. The ramp wound around on three different levels until finally we were in the church.

"Oh, I'm so glad you're here. I was beginning to worry," said a relieved Pastor Rachael O'Mera.

"God has a sense of divine timing, doesn't he?" I echoed. "I just need someone to help me get set up, pastor, and then we can go."

"Just come over by me when you are set to go. We will walk up the aisle together," replied the pastor.

We made the trek down the middle of the precious church. As I looked to my left and right I was warmed by all the smiles. How could someone from so far away be given such a nice welcome? They didn't even know me here.

No matter where I am, God gives me the courage to stand up for him, even in Dallas. The Lord revealed to me just months earlier to not take it personally if the people accept or reject my message. You see, the Holy Spirit is the one who does the talking, anyway. But, frankly, within minutes of being in Dallas I actually was feeling like family.

We continued down the aisle until Pastor O'Mera directed me to the front pew as she continued to walk up to the huge pulpit in the sanctuary. It became very quiet when the service started promptly at 10:45 A.M.

"Good morning, church. Today, we have with us a very special guest. His name is Steve Rose. He does a radio talk show with the Christians on the Green Bay Packers. We feel privileged to have had him come all this way to share his testimony of the mercy of the Lord Jesus Christ, and how it has led to a ministry with the Christians on the Super Bowl Champions."

When I heard those words, a spirit came over me which told me that I hadn't come all this way for nothing. "Something special was going to happen in Dallas this morning," I thought. Pastor continued.

"Steve is even going to try to convince us this morning that God may be a Packer fan!" You could hear a few snickers. I was confidant that they knew where I was coming from. And that's simply because where God is given His place, He'll move. They would soon agree that this was the case in Green Bay. A few of them did gasp when Pastor O'Mera said that, though. This reaction isn't all that unusual, really, no matter where I deliver my message of hope, help, and encouragement.

"After a few special numbers we will hear what Brother Steve has come all this way to share with us this morning."

Three godly men with voices like the Statler Brothers sang a song so beautiful I could have been convinced they were angels. They apologized that one of the regulars was missing and one of the gentlemen was a substitute. You could have fooled me.

The gentlemen singing that day were Roger Amdall, Rick Berg, and Dan Shackleton. The group is known in the Dallas area as "The

Lord's Men." I can see why. Soon they were finished, and within a couple minutes I'd get an idea of just how the congregation felt about a Packer fan in Dallas.

"Ladies and gentlemen of the Assembly of God in Dallas, will you please give Steve Rose a warm welcome this morning?"

After a nice smattering of applause, I stared out over the jammed-packed church. "Welcome to the *Leap of Faith* "Temporary Insanity" Book Tour! I guess today I can understand if we have a few Cowboy fans here," I laughed. "But I want you to know that *you*, my brothers and sisters in the Lord, supersede any differences we may have." I could tell already by this time that their lifestyle was very different from mine, but today I wasn't going to let that matter, if they wouldn't. This day we would all be one.

I shared the story of how I became involved with the Packers in ministry before I talked about how I had wasted my life for so many years before coming to the Lord in October of 1991.

"Life is such a gift," I told them. It was back in September of 1981 when I heard a story that really reached me with just how precious it is, and important it is, to appreciate our families.

"It was in Clarion, Iowa, in a place called Wayne's Tap, where a lady told me a story of her family. It was October of 1977 when her mom and dad, Rodney and Bonnie Lou, her sixteen-year-old sister Tracy, an absolute beauty queen, and her little brother Shannon left without her in the family plane on a Friday to visit relatives in Blair, Nebraska," I explained.

"At about 4:00 P.M. on Sunday they called to tell her they couldn't wait to pack up and come home. 'We will see you about six o'clock. Love you, see you then,' said her dad.

"At six they still weren't home. By eight, everyone in the little town of Clarion seemed to be over at the house waiting for them. At ten, someone offered to call the Federal Aviation to see if there was anything reported on radar. There wasn't."

At this point in my story, I noted a real sense of concern among the Dallas faithful. They were hungry for the rest of the story, and I gave them the final chapter.

"Well, the night before finally did turn into the morning after, when a doctor came to the door, introduced himself, and followed the lady—the one who told me this story—around the house," I continued.

"The phone eventually rang about 9:00 A.M. She says it was the most sickening, nauseating ring you would ever want to hear in your whole life. Now the doctor was sitting next to her and she says he took a needle out of his bag. Someone handed her the phone.

"The voice on the other end gave her the news she had been dreading to hear. 'Ma'am, this morning at about 7:30 a school bus driver from Blair happened to look off into a soybean field and spotted the wreckage of the plane.' She told me it wasn't like she didn't know it already. It was merely the confirmation of her greatest fear.

" 'It is with our deepest condolences and sympathy that we must tell you that you have lost your mother, father, brother, sister, and the family dog. Because of the trauma of their injuries, you will never see them again.' Right then, the doctor reached over and gave her the sedative, and she said she woke up a few hours later to a life that one can only begin to imagine," I finished.

In Tampa, Seattle, Milwaukee, even Dallas, everyone understands family, and together we all relived the shock and grief that woman felt.

"This is a very personal story to me," I continued, "because the one who told it to me, her name is Kim, and for the last fourteen years she's been my wife."

I know that it's just an expression, but you *could* have heard a pin drop in that place.

Kim's loss years ago touched the congregation in that church in Dallas, and we all cried a little afterwards. It is a day that will always live in my memory. The love of Jesus was on the faces of those people. Their hugs and handshakes afterwards had a feeling and emotion like I have never felt before.

It took about forty-five minutes to sign books in the church.

I recall meeting the Balts family. There was Jessica, Jolene, the boys, and mom and dad. I believe God had given me a word for Jolene as I said goodbye to her and her family in the parking lot.

"Jolene, I really feel God has a special plan for your life. The love of the Lord is all over you. God bless you."

"Thank you," she said.

By 12:30 I was waving to the Balts from the highway. My heart was very heavy as I suddenly missed my wife very much. I was lonely and I wished I could have been at home with her. I cried as I thought about her at home. There still was one more layover, and then I could go home.

Friends, I must tell you that I found some of the most wonderful people I have ever met, right there in Dallas. You really must know that some of the most caring, loving individuals I have ever come in contact with are in Dallas. And last, some of the greatest Packer fans I know are in Dallas. I wish you could have been with me the day the *Leap of Faith* "Temporary Insanity" book tour made a two-hour stop after a four-hour drive to the northern Wisconsin village of Dallas. That's right, I was in Dallas. Dallas, Wisconsin!

Dallas, Wisconsin, is about forty miles north of Eau Claire, just off Highway 53 on County Road A. John Peterson, the two-time medalist wrestler on the U.S.A. Olympic team, lives in nearby Comstock. He is a wrestling coach at Cumberland High School. My second stop that day was just south of Dallas, off of Highway 94 in Bloomer! I spoke at a gathering of youth there.

If you're ever in the area, be sure to join the Balts, Pastor O'Mera, and her loving congregation at the Assembly of God Church in Dallas, Wisconsin, for their 10:45 service. They'd love to see you. I can tell you that you'll receive a welcome like one can get . . . only in Dallas! The church is at 215 Second Avenue North. Phone 715 837-1661.

Chapter 14

Reggie's Prayer

Brett Favre is like a kid in a candy store. Wide-eyed and a tad nervous. He's in Green Bay and it's showtime. Mike Holmgren is standing next to him. Mike always thought about an acting career, especially after away games in the Metrodome. The unshaven Brett . . . looks like Brett. Coach—well, he looks like a janitor. Beause he is about to play one. And Favre is going to help him!

On this warm August day in 1996, Green Bay Notre Dame High School is turned into "Hollywood East." The quarterback and the coach have come to help a friend. The fact that the personal favor takes them out of their comfort zone is irrelevant. They believe in the project, which is the filming of a movie called "Reggie's Prayer." These will be the last shots for the film which began filming in May in Portland, Oregon. Some scenes were also shot in Knoxville, Tennessee.

We live in a world where we are barraged with jocks as pitchman for everything from credit cards to underwear. Are both of those products important? There probably are some who will agree that the removal of either can cause discomfort. But what about endorsing morality, values, and love? Wow, pretty dangerous subjects these days. But not for Reggie White.

In the serious fictional movie, White plays Reggie Knox, a retired football player who is inspired to reach out to teens. It's not some "jockudrama" to add to the list of his accomplishments, or to blaze a path to the big screen once he's done eating quarterbacks in Green Bay. So why did he and his family take an off-season to work instead of rest? For movie stardom? Reggie elaborated on that question.

"The message appealed to me. I was excited when I read the script because it was written based on my character, my Christian lifestyle, and lots of principles I believe in," he explained.

God bless Paul McKellips, the writer, producer, and director of the film. Paul grew up in nearby Neenah, Wisconsin, just thirty-five miles south of Green Bay. Today, Oregon is home. Is the fact that he loves the Packers the force behind wanting to use White and the Packer platform?

"Obviously, I'm a huge Packer fan," says McKellips. Being a fan, though, was only a small part of the motivation behind his first major feature film. "We wanted to do a film that showed the love of Christ and also showed a black man in a positive light. Why can't we have a black version of the Cleavers? Why does Hollywood continue to portray blacks as deviant?" he asked.

It may be apparent to many why White was chosen to help bring the Lord's message to light, but we asked McKellips anyway. "When you look at the country in regard to the lack of role models," he said, "and the current foundation of the family, I asked myself, 'Who has the greatest potential for uniting both blacks and whites, while positively impacting the family?'

"And we also wondered who is the person least likely to fall from grace by doing something crazy that would end up in the newspaper the next day? Who is at the top of our collective pedestal as far as maintaining the cause of the family? The answer I came up with is Reggie White." Good answer.

Reggie, Sara, and Jeremy and Jecolia White arrived in Portland for the shooting. All would have a part. Folks like Pat Morita ("The Karate Kid"); Paul "The Giant" Wight, M.C. Hammer, Rosey Grier, Bryce Paup, and teammate Keith Jackson would follow to help get the picture "in the can."

If you saw the movie, which was released in January of 1997, here's some of what you may have seen. You watched as White, who

Holmgren, McKellips, White, and Favre on the set of the filming of "Reggie's Prayer." (Used with permission. ©1997 Reggie White Studios, Inc. All rights reserved.)

plays Reggie Knox in the picture, stepped down as a professional player to become the head football coach and tenth-grade history teacher at Portland Central High. Morita would help Knox in his frustrating journey to help disadvantaged kids.

You felt for Knox as he had nightmares about a teen suicide and an accidental shooting in the team locker room, which left a boy critically wounded. You may have felt embraced by the adventure of White out in the wilderness where he battled Paul "The Giant" while pursuing a criminal and a teenage hostage. There are also some unforgettable moments that weren't caught on film but that may also have eternal value, just as those of the picture itself.

On the last day of shooting the scenes in Portland, Paul McKellips asked White if he wanted to say anything to the kids who were cast for the history class scenes, mostly African-American inner-city high school kids. There were even gang members there. McKellips explained why.

"Our message is one that says there are opportunities for teenagers in the world. We wanted to practice what we preached, so we invited the members from a gang to be with us," noted the director. "But there was a limitation. We didn't invite members from two gangs. That would not have been wise!"

Off camera, after the filming, White boldly talked to the girls in the classroom about virginity and virtues. The approach to the guys was forthright, as well.

"Guys, making love doesn't make you a man. Learn to love everything you make. That's what's important. Fellas, one of the biggest problems we face is that our women have been carrying us. For too long too many of our men are in prison, on probation, or just gone from the family. It needs to turn around with your generation."

Paul McKellips recalls just what a powerful moment it was as the gentle giant spoke. "Within a couple minutes of when Reggie began to address those kids, there wasn't an eyeball that was dry in the room, including mine."

"Reggie's Prayer" may be one of few movies which has had the benefit of a prayer intercessor for every day of shooting. This is someone praying for the project and that it would be used for God's glory, not man's. That would inspire many to embrace God's message of love and forgiveness through Christ.

The last day of shooting in Portland finished at 4:00 A.M. Reggie had accepted an offer to speak at a local high school at breakfast that morning. Because he'd been up all night, McKellips assumed White probably would want to postpone the breakfast appearance. Forget that idea.

"I asked Reggie if he wanted me to call and let them know he wouldn't be able to make it." He was quite surprised when White retorted, "Tell them, *we'll* be there! What time are *you* gonna pick me up?" Reggie was on time to speak to fifteen kids that morning and even recruited an exhausted director to drive him.

In preparation for the Green Bay shoot with Favre and Holmgren, the crew jetted to "Titletown USA." On Sunday, August 18, 1996, Coach Holmgren walked into Green Bay Notre Dame High School.

Gretta McKellips, Paul's mother, had come for the shooting. She remembers meeting the special men. "Coach went to shake my hand and I told him, 'I don't shake hands with head coaches, I only take hugs!'"

He obliged. "He's a great hugger," she said after the shoot. Mrs. McKellips, 77, also made Favre blush as he burst into laughter during a picture taken later when she asked him, "How would you like to propose to a much older woman?"

Mike Holmgren said shortly after his arrival, "I have two hours before I have to go look at film. Let's do it." The Packers had played the Baltimore Ravens the day before and it was something of a minor miracle that he was graciously taking the time to help.

Holmgren looked grandfatherish with his hair greased back. He wore bifocals and a blue janitor outfit, and he leaned on a mop as he was instructed to do. He would play a janitor at the school where White was coaching.

Brett Favre is a cool customer when 300-pound lineman stalk him looking to crunch his bones, but in front of a camera—well he had butterflies like any other actor. Paul McKellips elaborated.

"He was kind of scared. After all, he's a football player, not an actor. It was really crazy having a guy of his magnitude looking at me with a little bit of fright in his eyes. He was paying attention to me like a student in class. Then he knocked my socks off. The kid can act. He did a Foster Brooks impersonation in rehearsal that sold me."

In the scene with Holmgren and Favre, White is passing through the hallway outside the locker room. As Holmgren leans on his mop he suggests to Reggie that he use a play he and his son invented years ago. Holmgren calls the play his "left coast special." The burly lineman turned actor sort of "laughed it off." After all, what did the janitor know about football anyway?

Favre, who plays Holmgren's son, Burt, is unpacking some toilet paper to assist his dad.

As White leaves the scene to coach his first high school game, Holmgren says to Favre, "Hey, you got a pretty good arm, don't you, Burt?"

Favre deadpans, "I coulda played."

Holmgren sneers at his two-time MVP and hands him the broom. "Yeah, right. Finish up the sweeping. I gotta change the urinal mints."

Chapter 15

Home Sweet Holmgren

On the sidelines, Coach Mike Holmgren is like General Patton. His men listen attentively to all of his words. Then they carry out the plan. He is in complete control. Is it possible for this man of God to take this sort of unquestioned leadership home to his family? Are you kidding?

According to his daughter, Jenny, "Dad likes to order for everyone when we go to a restaurant. When we order for ourselves, he goes into this 'martyr man' routine. We have learned to work around him."

It was a privilege to talk with Jenny Holmgren-Cobbley about her family. She was very open and candid with me about what it's like to be a part of this community, one that is literally fused together by the team. I know you'll enjoy her warmth. She acknowledges it hasn't always been easy being part of such a prominent family.

"When Dad became head coach of the Packers, everyone in the family knew that our lives would change," said Jenny. "At first, the attention was mostly fun, little things. We could go into the video store by our house without a rental card because they recognized us. We would get great service at restaurants and automotive shops. We got lots of boxes of chocolate at Christmas." As hard as it is to believe, even chocolate can get a little old after a while.

Meet the Holmgrens. Mom and Dad have been married twenty-six years. Jenny and Calla are twenty-two-year-old twin sisters. Then there is Emily, nineteen, and Gretchen, fifteen. Oh, and there are also two little dogs, Tiger and Lilly, who terrorize the neighborhood.

This family arrived in Green Bay in 1992, with Dad accepting a position with a lot of potential—for grief, if he wasn't successful. Fortunately, that hasn't been the case. As a matter of fact, it's been a textbook case of rising success every year. (What is the coach going to do for an encore?)

Before setting up house here, the Holmgrens lived in San Jose, California. Mike was the offensive coordinator for the San Francisco 49ers. Life was much different. For instance, he had to drive forty minutes one way to San Francisco for practice. This is a far cry from the few minutes it can take to get from his present home to Lambeau Field.

So, how do the Holmgrens like it here?

Jenny says, "It's a very nice community-oriented area. In San Francisco, everybody is going in a different direction." So, what is it like to be the part of the "first family" of the Green Bay Packers? Jenny tells us.

"Even though my dad's job as coach of the Packers is atypical, we actually have a normal routine for life during the season. On Mondays and Tuesdays, Dad works late studying film and constructing the game plan. On Wednesdays he is home by 7:30 P.M." It gets a little more exciting as the week goes on.

"Thursday night is family night because Dad is home for dinner—no one is allowed to do anything but be with the family. Mom and dad go out on a date on Friday night. On Saturday we order pizza, and Sunday is game day."

What, may we ask, happens on game day at the Holmgren house? Do the girls knit, do schoolwork, or shop?

"We're at Lambeau Field for the home games, but rarely go on road trips. This is partly because we'd drive each other nuts," Jenny explains.

The women of the house all have different personalities, and this is never more apparent than on game day, when the team is playing on the road and they watch at home on TV.

"Gretchen is the only one who likes to listen to the commentators. Emily gets angry if someone says negative things about the players, and Calla shrieks at the top of her lungs during fumbles and interceptions," smiles Jenny.

She continues, "Mom discovered she suffers from high blood pressure, a condition drastically aggravated by watching Packer games. It used to be enough to stay home and clean house, but now she has started walking around the neighborhood listening to relaxation tapes and church sermons."

Surely one could assume that the girls are all unshakable optimists when it comes to the Packers. Think again.

"I only saw the first half of the San Francisco playoff game out there," confessed Jenny. "With the score at 21-3, I was convinced something bad was going to happen, so I stuck "Steel Magnolias" in the VCR. I turned up the volume really loud. Ahh, but we won!" she recalled.

She noted there was another special thing about the 49ers game.

"Because the 49ers game was on a Saturday, we were able to go to church together as a family on Sunday. Church is a good place for Dad because you're supposed to be thinking about things more important than the Packers."

But usually, Jenny says, the insanity escalates during the playoffs. Then, nearly all semblance of normality for the family routine goes out the window. For example, the 1995 season was really wild.

One can only imagine that the Holmgrens had to wonder, along with the rest of us, just who came up with the idea to mix Christmas and football? That wasn't very smart. In 1995, the Packers-Steelers game on Christmas Eve almost caused a family breakdown at Holmgren Grand Central.

While the coach was busy trying to figure out a way to score enough points to beat the Steelers, Mom was doing everything else— buying gifts, setting up the tree, and organizing the Christmas cards the family had received.

A few days before the celebration of the birth of Christ, dad is asking, "Did we send out the Christmas cards already?"

"Mike, we never took a family picture," Mom answers.

"Yes, we did. We took it at Thanksgiving."

Mom looks at Jenny.

"Jenny, do you remember taking a family picture at Thanksgiving?" She shakes her head—no. It was definitely a playoff conversation.

Most of the weirdness in the Holmgren house is not due to the arrival of famous people—which happens often enough—it is usually caused by interaction between family members. However, there have been a few exceptions. During the '95 season, ESPN's Chris Berman (the guy with all the nicknames) dropped in for supper. Mrs. H. served up a family favorite, Chicken Lombardi, a tribute to the Packer legend.

"Do you girls know about football?" Berman asked the daughters.

"He should have asked Gretchen," says Jenny. "She would have given him a diagram of the nickel screen."

Gretchen and Jenny will never forget what happened during a late-night visit in December of 1995. Jenny recalls evesdropping on an interesting conversation.

"I was getting out of the shower. Gretchen came to my room and said, 'Don't go downstairs in your robe.'"

"Why not?"

"Reggie White is in the living room."

Such visits are not unusual. But this visit, as every Packer fan knows, was different. Reggie, out for the year a day earlier, had come to tell the coach his injured hamstring was on the mend, and that he might, somehow, play on Sunday.

"Gretchen and I shamelessly perched ourselves on the stairway and listened. Hey, we're Packer fans, too," said Jenny with a laugh.

There is one facet of this special group of individuals, who just happen to be from the same family, that bears emphasizing. They have a very strong faith, and it starts at the top. I recall the stories that talked about the coach's faith. It didn't make too many headlines, because much of the media was much more interested in learning how he proposed to bring the Lombardi trophy back to Green Bay.

However, the media and fans couldn't help but notice the "Packer pendulum" really began to swing once Holmgren took the helm. There may be more outspoken Christians on the team, but the coach walks the walk with any of them. Where did it all start for him, his walk with the Lord? The coach remembers.

"When I was eleven, Billy Graham held a three-week crusade at the Cow Palace in San Francisco. On the final night, while Cliff Barrows led the audience in singing "Just as I Am," I couldn't stay seated. I went forward to accept Christ just as I was, grubby tennis shoes and all."

Later, Holmgren was drafted by the St. Louis Cardinals football team in 1970. He was released and signed as a backup for Joe Namath on the New York Jets. He was eventually cut again.

A girl he had met at Mission Springs Bible Camp the summer after he became a Christian re-emerged in his life. She would later become his wife.

"Although we had corresponded off and on between summer reunions at camp, our friendship had cooled. Kathy had taken her faith much more seriously than I. But her inspiring letters helped me to realize how much I needed to trust the Lord in the midst of my disillusionment."

That was a key time for the young man who eventually would become the head coach of a Super Bowl Championship team. He explains.

"I recommitted my life to Christ. Proverbs 3:5-6 became the personal line of scrimmage at which I dug in. 'Trust in the Lord with all your heart, and lean not on your own understanding. In all of your ways acknowledge Him and He will make your path straight.'"

Steve and Kathy married in 1971. After a stint in San Francisco with the 49ers as an assistant coach, the call came to come to Green Bay, and as they say, the rest is history.

Mike is quick to point out that it hasn't always been easy. "Win or lose, I learned a long time ago what really matters. It's not Super Bowl rings, but the crown of eternal life Christ has won for us by His victory on the cross."

The man has his priorities in order. After the Super Bowl he made the decision to pass on paid appearances, speeches, and autograph shows after making a speech in Milwaukee in February. On the way back to Green Bay, Holmgren had to soothe his daughter Gretchen by cellular phone as he made the two-hour drive home. "You can't make up time. That was my last speech."

Nothing exemplifies Mike's commitment more than the following story, which you might never have heard before. The Packers had just nipped the Pittsburgh Steelers on Christmas Eve, 1995. Who can forget the infamous "Yancy Thigpen drop?" It propelled the team to their first Central Division championship in twenty-two years and gave them a home playoff game. The team was huddled around Holmgren in the locker room, just minutes after the win.

"Guys, we have given some gifts to other teams, but today we received a gift [Thigpen's dropped pass]. Let's remember the greatest gift of all, and that's the gift of Jesus Christ. That's the reason for the season. Have a Merry Christmas," he said solemnly, as he turned and walked away.

Meanwhile, Kathy Holmgren was waiting outside with several hundred excited Packer fans.

"Ree-gie, Ree-gie, Brett, Brett!" they yelled.

"I have to get through," she said. "I am Kathy Holmgren and I am my husband's ride home."

"Yeah, right," said the man next to her, rolling his eyes

You gotta love the excitement of Green Bay Packer football, except if you're a member of the Holmgren family, and then it can sometimes drive you bonkers.

Chapter 16

What? A Packer Family Fight?

I was beginning to wonder whether the Packer family was the Cleaver family. They were beginning to make me feel kind of uncomfortable. You know, until this year, I thought they never had fights and squabbles. We sure do in my family. In the spring of 1997 we learned, from the inside and out, that everybody really is human in the Packer organization.

Now, I'm usually not deep in my explanations and observations. That's probably because I am not the most highly educated guy and maybe a little shallow as a person. But the events of the past off-season, and the hullabaloo surrounding the White House trip and Super Bowl ring fiasco, are worth delving into. I really don't know what happened.

Here's what was reported. There were some former Packers who were not invited to go to the White House to see the president. This trip is traditional in professional sports after a world championship is won. Then there was a similar situation with the scheduled Super Bowl ring ceremony.

As many of you can probably tell by now, in both this book and the previous volume, *Leap of Faith: God Must Be A Packer Fan*, we do everything we can to avoid controversy. With that in mind, I considered not addressing this whole issue. Then something told me that would be noticed and throw me into denial. Hey, it happened. Let's take a look at the situation. Not to wound, but to heal.

I've called in an expert for this one. I do have to admit, besides being an author and speaker, I'd like to do some marriage counseling. When I shared this desire with my wife, I thought she was gonna fall over dead from laughter. Said it was the funniest thing she'd ever heard. Frankly I was kind of offended by that. So was my shrink.

Speaking of my shrink, I thought she'd be perfect to decipher and dissect this whole Packer family conflict. Maybe you remember her. She is Packerwomaniac and a licensed marriage and family therapist, Donna Morgan. (She's the one from Chapter 4 who talks to her TV during Packer games. Hey, good help is hard to find, OK?)

She is great in her field. She's not perfect in her personal life, though. She makes mistakes, just like the rest of us. I don't want to tell you she's not had her share of problems in her past. She did tell me once, years ago, that she called the suicide hotline. After she told them her problems, somebody there told her, "Lady, you know, maybe jumping off a cliff wouldn't be the worst thing for you!"

Her husband, Bob, came in and rescued her and her life has been bliss ever since. As the Bible says, "Behind every good woman is a good man." Okay, maybe it doesn't say that, but it should.

I think you'll like what she has seen here in the "Packer Family Squabble." Chew the meat and spit out the bones. There really isn't a way anyone can be right all the time. Nobody bats a thousand on any team, even the Packers. Donna, incidentally, really is a licensed therapist.

The following is some of her take on the whole situation that arose during the post Super Bowl off-season. Keep in mind her observations are for entertainment purposes only, but I think she makes some great points.

She says, "Because God is a Packer fan doesn't mean the Packer family is perfect. We're *all* God's children and none of us is perfect. The Packer family is made up of many different people in many roles. They all do some good things and some careless things. They're just like the rest of us."

Isn't this comforting to know?

Let's meet and take a look at the Packer family.

Parent #1	**Parent #2**
Packer Administration	Packer Fans

The Kids
Packer Players

Donna will help us try to look at the Packer organization as a family unit, just like yours and mine.

"Try to think of the whole organization and the fans as a family. (See the diagram above.) Parent #1 is the Packer Administration. Parent #2 is the Packer fans. The Packer players are the kids of the family. They are kids, after all. The average age is probably only in the mid-twenties."

I liked what Jerry Kramer pointed out in the foreword to Jerry Poling's book, *Downfield*. He said, "Remember the next time a player makes a spectacular play, it's no more or less than we're all capable of. Remember the next time a player screws up—they are boys playing a game."

Even the men of the family screw up. We know this today.

The Packer organization has really been pretty blessed over the years, according to Donna.

"The Packer family has functioned pretty well. They have for a long time. For the most part, with some exceptions, they play as a team— not as a group of individuals. They've been supportive of each other and encouraged each other's growth. They usually communicate very effectively."

However, there are other requisites for success, and Donna sees some big ones in the Packer camp.

"In order to win a Super Bowl, flexibility is necessary. So is hard work and unity. These are signs of a healthy family. When things go very well with our team, we're happy. It makes it very easy to love the family.

"Then we are in awe of the family. But when problems arise and communication doesn't flow as it should, some careless things can get said. During these times some decisions are made that can hurt all or part of the family.

"When this happens in our precious Packer family, we sometimes are shocked and disillusioned. We discover that they're not flawless. We are then often quick to criticize."

Donna Morgan, family therapist and Packerwomaniac.

Donna continues. "Looking at errors in judgment and behavior is not the way to evaluate a family. The true test of a healthy family is how they survive the tests of conflict, disagreements, outside interference, and other challenging situations. Communicating feelings to one another and trying to understand each other's positions is a key."

Again, flexibility comes up.

"If all sides can be flexible enough to make changes to correct the problem, then they are a healthy family, and usually a happy family."

Delicately, let's look back at what happened in May of 1997 in Green Bay, when fans burned up the phone lines calling the Packer offices. Newspapers had to buy additional thousands of pounds of paper to cover it all.

Refer to your diagram as Donna Morgan, guest licensed football family therapist, continues. Again, this is for entertainment purposes only. (But that doesn't mean she isn't right!)

"Somewhere along the line, in the distant or not too distant past, Parent #1 (Packer administration) may have got its feelings hurt by a kid or two (a player)."

In this case, Donna is referring to the Chris Jacke case, Desmond Howard's leaving the team, and the departure of a couple of the guys who were free agents. We need to point out that Parent #1 made its decision with no explanation to Parent #2 (the fans) and the kids. It probably is a whole other debate whether an explanation was warranted or not. But because of the high profile of the organization, it seems that it's tougher to keep things internal, even things that deserve to remain internal. With that brought to the table, Donna Morgan, crack football family therapist continues.

"It appears that Parent #1 perceived a lack of respect, loyalty, and gratefulness on behalf of a few of the kids. After all, any parent who has given what they believe is their all to their youngsters (and this administration does) expects some things in return. In most families, however, parents rarely get this return on their investment until the kids have grown up and moved away. Many times, only then do they realize just how smart mom and dad have gotten!"

Parents, ask yourself, "Have you always gotten the respect, loyalty, and gratitude you felt you deserved while the kids were still at home?" *Not!*

Donna adds, "In this case the hurting Parent (#1) retaliated by not letting any youngster who was leaving the family (whether by choice of their own or not) participate in the family trip to the White House." We all can relate to Donna's next axiom: "Discipline decisions made too quickly and out of hurt or anger are rarely good decisions."

Isn't that a great point? We all can ask, "Have our parents or those of us as parents ever made judgments too quickly? Maybe handed out our version of justice without a good night's sleep to think about it first?"

The therapist digs deeper into the debacle. "On the day the team went to the White House, a lot of people hurt. Some of the kids who went to the White House were hurt, too. Parent #2 (the Packer fans) hurt, too, and seeing the suffering of the kids, felt angered and wounded." The next is her strongest statement up to this point. "I really believe, on that day, we saw the Packer family functioning at its lowest point.

"Parent #2 had now watched enough, especially knowing there were a few of the kids who weren't invited to to either the White House reception or the Super Bowl ring ceremony in June."

Here's what transpired after Parent #2 was informed of this. We watched and listened as the Parents 1 & 2 had a standoff. And it wasn't nice to watch. For a couple weeks, on TV, in the newspapers, and on the radio, it got downright ugly.

Parent #2 buried Parent #1 with requests to allow one of the kids, Chris Jacke, to take part in the ring ceremony. Parent #1 bent as Parent #2 convinced them to be more flexible. But don't expect Parent #1 to admit that they were wrong, and were set right only by the other parent. Parent #1 released this statement:

"As we reviewed our decision we feel it [the decision] was appropriate. But because we listen to our fans, we decided to change it."

Was this a way of saying, "We got tired of our phone ringing, our fax burning up, and hearing all those bad things about us on radio, on TV, in the newspapers, and on the street." Well, we'll never know, and really, Parent #2 probably doesn't care. They got what they wanted for the kid [Jacke].

The kid was happy, too. Here's what Chris had to say a week after he had gotten his ring. "I'm glad it's over. It got bigger than I ever thought it would get. But the fan support has been just awesome. I'm real pleased the way it turned out."

While some have argued that the entire situation was blown out of proportion, Chris doesn't think that's the case. "I don't want to say that because fan support was so good. I don't want to belittle what they did. It just shows that the fans (Parent #2) support the players and the players [the kids] support the fans. There's give and take there and I'm glad the fans voiced their opinions and the administration listened."

Just for argument's sake and to keep somewhat of a score, even a one-time kid got into the action. Fuzzy Thurston, a star Packers offensive guard who played key roles in Super Bowls I and II, came to Jacke's defense.

"I think even though he wasn't any longer a Packer, he should have been allowed to go to the party." Fuzzy said further that this should also have been the case with Desmond Howard and Andre Rison. Howard was later invited and did show up, but not without some animosity. "I have to admit, it has dampened my view of this organization," he noted.

For the most part, everyone survived the whole hullabaloo. Donna puts a few finishing touches on this learning experience.

"For the most part, the parents communicated lovingly, rationally, and effectively. Even in hard times the love affair between the Packers administration, players, and fans still goes on. They shared their feelings, attitudes, and thoughts about all the decisions that were made and their consequences. Ultimately, it led to the administration being flexible enough to change its mind. This is a sign of a healthy family. The wounds will heal."

Aww . . . you can almost feel the hugs of the love affair again, can't you? This probably won't ever happen again. Yeah, right. Just wait and see what happens when Brett or Reggie gets sent to bed without supper!

Chapter 17

God Bless the Media

There was the mountain of a man, Reggie White, on TV, talking about God again. "I want to thank the Lord, Jesus Christ and give Him the glory for this victory," said White, plunging his fist in the air. Loudly, sixty thousand people in Lambeau Field for the NFC Championship echoed their approval.

Not too long ago, a network wouldn't have allowed such a proclamation. They would have shrieked, shunned, and cringed while cutting away to shove the microphone in somebody else's face. Well, God bless those in the media standing up for the faithful! And God will bless those media outlets that are not offended to report the good news—the big picture.

This may come as a huge surprise to you, but most of the media covering the NFL care only about statistics. That's right—touchdowns, interceptions, and fumbles. They really don't care to have their newspapers, radio, or TV waves littered with how the Almighty is moving on the court, diamond, ice, or field. Many would much rather take a chance of having a hungry Mike Tyson whisper in their ear, than interview one of those "religious jocks" who profess Christ. One reporter told me, "There are a lot of people in newsrooms who avoid

Christian coverage because they want to avoid controversy. They feel uncomfortable reporting it."

As I listen to Reggie and the other guys, through the media, I am reminded of one thing: There is only one reason why I have been able to write this book. And that is because we have some very gutsy, faithful people in Green Bay—who just happen to play football. This book is in your hand because of some equally bold radio, TV, and newspaper types who haven't been offended by God's message.

I believe that message is that God is up to something directly relating to the Green Bay Packers. I am totally convinced that football is the platform for Reggie and the Packers. That's it. In ten minutes, Christ could rapture us out of here, and my bet is that all the Vince Lombardi trophies and Super Bowl rings will then be left behind.

How long has it been since the TV cameras have shown prayer on the 50-yard line? You're right. It's been only in the last few years. How about the John 3:16 signs that pop out of the masses in the end zone? Why is this happening now? It's because of God alone, and He *will* honor media people and anyone who will report the good news of Christ's love. "The sacred and secular are merging," said Michele Dillon, a Yale University professor of religion.

At the risk of leaving out too many people, I am going to talk about a few very faithful media folks who are not the least bit reluctant to share their faith and feelings, and who freely express how they feel that God is being glorified through this team.

Few will argue that Reggie White's miraculous healings opened the door to separate the believers from the nonbelievers in Packerland. Mike Vandermause, Assistant Sports Editor of the *Milwaukee Journal Sentinel*, is one of the believers. He hasn't shied away from talking about God in the lives of the Packers. He has taken a fascinating stance and made some golden comments after White's hamstring injury in 1995.

"I suppose it's a natural human response to search for a rational explanation when something miraculous occurs," said Mike. "The most asked question from doubters seems to be, 'Doesn't God have more important things to do than heal a football player's hamstring?'

"The way I see it, God cares for all his children, and Reggie White is one of them. Why is it so hard to believe that God would choose to further his purposes by using White, a very prominent man with a faith that can move mountains?"

Is Reggie White something extraordinary? Vandermause seems to think so. He continues to share his feeling about the blast of the miraculous through big number 92. "There's something very special about White. He's bold in proclaiming his faith, but doesn't push it down people's throats. He chooses not to bask in the spotlight."

Vandermause confirmed that some reporters roll their eyes or turn off their tape recorders when a player starts giving credit to God. But it's different with White. He's sincere, and his words can't be ignored. He *is* one big powerful package, and he's impossible to ignore. Vandermause wraps up his case with one pithy sentence: "It would take more faith not to believe that God would choose to work through an individual as unique as White."

Weeknights on radio AM 1130, WISN in Milwaukee, Steve True hosts "The World's Greatest Talk Show." He, too, has no doubts or fears of delving into the obvious. Last October 23rd I was thrilled to be a "gust," I mean, *guest*. He jumped right into the spiritual side of things, which really impressed me.

"Why the title, *God Must be A Packer Fan?*" he asked.

"Steve, what we're saying here is that where God is given His place He will move. That certainly is happening in Green Bay," I answered.

We talked about Reggie's hamstring injury in 1995. I told him this healing, after Reggie's '94 elbow injury, really was the final impetus that got me to write the book.

"You mean the one about the 'born-again hamstring?'" he quipped. "I consider my faith to be strong, but I'll admit, and I even told Reggie, at times the healings get to be a little much," he confessed. His next point was well taken.

"If I played on another team, I would be a bit offended. I would think God is a Viking's fan, if I was Chris Carter. Or, should everyone just respect the impact faith has had the lives of these players and the lives of those they've touched? Is there a risk of going too far?"

The Lord says we should be wise as serpents and harmless as doves. But sometimes we need to be a little bolder than our comfort zone can handle. I doubt if Reggie has any fears about crossing the line. It sure doesn't look as if he's concerned about what anybody thinks.

Tom Pipines, of WITI TV-6.

"But it's a real credit to Reggie White to how open people are to the faith aspect," pointed out True. "Because you know talking to athletes in the past, it was something they weren't real comfortable talking about. The Packers, through Reggie White, have kind of destroyed that."

He made a great point about an article that had recently run in a Wisconsin newspaper. He didn't identify the paper. I wish he would have, so they could have been recognized. If you find it, let me know, please. We'll give them special mention in the third book of this trilogy. Here's what True said about this specific article:

"I'll guarantee you," he started. "This has never been done in the history of the media. The first question the reporter asked of [Packer fullback] William Henderson was, 'I heard recently that you have accepted Jesus Christ as your Savior.' What interview ever started that way? If it was towards the end, OK." Great point.

Tom Pipines, from Milwaukee WITI TV-6, has some feelings about why the Lord may have chosen the Packers as a vessel for communication. "I believe God honors any man or woman who seeks Him. God has given athletes the gifts to excel. He loves to see these individuals get the most out of their talent. The progress is commensurate with their spiritual lives and hard work," notes Tom.

Meet Richard Wood, a photographer for the *Milwaukee Journal Sentinel*. He believes there's a bigger picture than the one he's shooting or seeing. "I've covered the Packers when they weren't so popular," he said. "During the Gregg and Infante years, it wasn't as much fun as now. Bob Harlan has really added a personal touch. He is a very principled man, making principled decisions."

I know that sometimes we, along with the media, are guilty of getting on our high horses, picking on the other guys and teams about their problems, but Rick reminds us that things were different here, not too long ago.

"Years ago, there used to be a joke during upcoming NFL drafts. People would ask, 'Who should the Packers draft this year?' and the answer would be, 'A defensive lawyer,'" he laughed. A subtle reminder that we shouldn't take any satisfaction in the misfortune of others. We should remember that we've had plenty of our own over the years.

So why does Rick think the Lord is moving in Green Bay? "Here's a situation where a small market was ripe for God to move. God loves Packer fans because they are faithful and loyal. Those are fruits of the spirit (Galatians 5:20). These fans had to believe before they could see!"

He dug deeper. "What prompted some of the guys over the years to stay in Green Bay when they could have made more money elsewhere? One word—relationships." All one needs to do is read the articles to find this has been the case with some of the free agents in Green Bay.

Green Bay TV personality Bill Jartz was right. In my first book, before the Packers had won the Super Bowl, Jartz made a prophetic statement: "Packer fans are knowledgeable and classy." He was amazed at the depth of feeling of Packer fans all over the country, a depth that I believe shows the hand of God on the hearts of Packer fans.

Jartz knew the Packers were on the verge of something great. "The next step will be the big one," he told me. "When we win the Super Bowl, there will be no Detroit-type riots in Green Bay." Remarkably, tens of thousands were well behaved as three buses brought the team through the crowded streets of Green Bay on the way to a celebration at Lambeau Field. It was called "Return to Titletown."

Listen to the following story. Is it coincidence or God-incidence?

It's the morning of Super Bowl XXXI. Rick Wood, the *Journal Sentinel* photographer mentioned earlier, has his Bible tucked under his arm as he walks by some of his colleagues from the *Milwaukee Journal Sentinel* who are sitting around the hotel pool. He finds a place to pray and read.

Hours later, in the stadium, as Coach Holmgren is being carried from the field in victory, Wood lifts his camera above his head. Without seeing Holmgren, pointing his camera as best he can—click, click, click—he fires away. He cannot see Holmgren at all. The picture turns out to be a classic.

You may recall the shot with Holmgren on the shoulders of those lovable Packers. Confetti is flying overhead. Coincidence or God-incidence? His *Journal Sentinel* colleagues feel it was the latter. "Ricky, we believe you got that picture because you were praying that morning."

In the same way God has blessed many on the Packers who feel it's "cool" to be a Christian, I know He will honor the stand of people like Mike Vandermause, Steve True, Tom Pipenes, Rick Wood, and Bill Jartz. Ditto to the hundreds of others in the media not mentioned here, the ones who are bold enough to point out there is more . . . much more, but it can only be seen through spiritual eyes.

Chapter 18

"Pittsville"

By Bob Gardinier

It was "pittsville." That's how November 20, 1996, will be remembered by many Packer fans, including Steve Rose and me. At about 6:30 that night I was playing cashier at Steve's book table. Up walked a man who looked to be in his early 60s. The news he gave us fell like a bombshell. Within seconds after this stranger's four-word announcement, our night was sent on a whole new course. As matter of fact, I *can* tell you that Steve Rose's ministry has never been the same since.

In church on the previous Sunday, Pastor Bill Myers from First Assembly in Appleton looked out over approximately five hundred of us seated in the sanctuary and asked, "Is Steve Rose here?" Steve later told me he wanted to bolt for the door. The sermon that morning had hit him right between the eyes. Steve was seated near the end of a pew and, hesitating, stepped out into the aisle.

Pastor Myers looked right at him and boldly yet lovingly proclaimed, "We want to pray that your book will save souls!" Pastor Myers, like so many others, wants to see the world saved for Christ.

After the service, Steve came over to my wife, Linda, and my son, Andy, who had been sitting with me. We stood and chatted for a few minutes. Then Steve asked me if I'd like to go along with him to Pittsville, Wisconsin, on the following Wednesday. He was scheduled to do a high school assembly program there in the afternoon, and an evangelical rally for the community in the evening.

I found this unusual, because when Steve is on the road, I usually cover for him at his office. So it surprised me when he made the offer to join him.

"Bob, I really feel in my heart that you should be in Pittsville with me on Wednesday," he told me. "You could drive for me and help me with the books and stuff."

With his hectic schedule, I could see that simply having someone drive occasionally would be a real blessing to him. I looked at Linda and she shrugged her shoulders as if to say, "OK by me." I said, "Let me give it some thought, but I don't see why I can't."

The next morning I called Steve to tell him I had made all necessary arrangements to join the *Leap of Faith* book tour stop in Pittsville.

At 10:30 on Wednesday morning, we were breezing east on Highway 10, on our way to Pittsville. We stopped at a little diner in Plover for lunch and continued the journey through Wisconsin Rapids and Port Edwards. We wound around some narrow backroads, admiring the scenery.

"Man, how would you like to drive these winding roads during a snow storm?" I quizzed my friend. Little did we know we would be doing just that, about nine hours later.

By 1:30 we had arrived at Pittsville High School. Principal John Olig introduced himself to us. By 2:15 the students were piling into the gym, and then Steve began his presentation. The students were very receptive to his message. He connects with audiences, including teenagers, because he does everything he can to relate to them. He builds a bridge. This day was no different.

"Have any of you guys ever fallen asleep in study hall?" he asked.

I could tell by the grins and blushed faces, he'd connected.

"Don't you just hate that when the bell rings, and you wake up with drool hanging off your lower lip?"

"Aawwww!" they groaned and giggled. It's stuff like that he does to let them know he has been there himself. He has felt their fears, hurts, and anxieties. And he can make them laugh. There's a saying that says, "People don't care how much you know, till they know how much you care," and Steve lets his audiences know he cares.

"I believe in you guys!" said Steve. "Choose the road of self-discipline. My friends, Robert Brooks and Ken Ruettgers are reminders to me that you will never see a champion without self-discipline. It can't happen. Don't go down the shortcut road of hell and heartbreak, like I did," he pleaded. "You can make your dream happen—but it takes work."

Steve used the example of a Pittsville High alum who had won four state wrestling championships. He had seen a picture of him that day in the school's trophy case. "I can tell you without even knowing this student that he was a hard worker. He was the first one in the weight room, the last to leave. Success isn't an accident."

He continued. "If a person can screw up as bad as I have and still have their dreams come true, imagine what *you* can accomplish in *your* life, if you'll believe there is a great plan for you, and then do something about it."

After thirty minutes, Steve wrapped it up.

"You guys were great. I hope you will come back out tonight for the rally. Go Packers and Pittsville Panthers!"

He was given a warm ovation as he exited off to the left and out the door into the hallway where some faculty members greeted him. I tell you, even if the students didn't appreciate him, the teachers sure do. He affirms and confirms everything they teach.

We gave away a couple books and chatted with some of the people who were in charge of the festivities for the evening to come.

"Welcome to Pittsville, the geographical center of the state," we were told, as we proceeded to Pastor Bruce Naugle's for supper. As we were seated at the supper table, I remember Steve asking Pastor Naugle, "Should I do an alter call tonight?"

"I'll leave that up to you," Pastor replied.

We ate heartily. Wow, what a pistachio pie Mrs. Naugle made for us! Almost as good as my wife's!

It was snowing fairly heavy as we drove back to the high school. The windshield wipers were flapping time as we discussed the game plan for the talk and the book signing. We were set up and signing books by six o'clock.

"Could I get your autograph, too?" a little girl said to me, after getting Steve to sign her book. She must have thought I was important since I was helping Steve.

"Why not?" I thought to myself as I obliged her.

Then came the news. We'd been totally separated from the world all day and hadn't heard a sports report. And here was the man with the four words. He was chatting with Steve as he signed his book. Neither of us were ready for his next words.

"Your buddy retired today, huh?"

"Pardon me?" said Steve with a confused look on his face.

"Ken Ruettgers retired today."

The guy must have thought we knew about it. We hadn't. I saw the color leave Steve's face. He told me later it felt like somebody kicked him in the chest.

"Really?" Steve remarked. "I didn't know that. When did they make the announcement?"

"They had a press conference in Green Bay this afternoon."

Steve later told me that it really wasn't the surprise so much as the sudden realization that football was over for his friend Ken Ruettgers. I could tell Steve was choked up. I mean, here was his radio partner and friend announcing that his career was history. Both of us and about a hundred million other people knew the Packers were headed to the Super Bowl. Why Lord, why now? Why won't Ken be playing in the Super Bowl?

I knew Steve was hurting, but he was still in rare form as he spoke to a crowd of about a hundred.

"I was a victim of child abuse," he told them.

It was dead-silent for a moment, and then Steve sprang the joke.

"No, Mom and Dad didn't hit me or anything. I had to work on the family farm, and I think that must be the purest form of child abuse there is." The audience got a kick out of that.

"Anybody here come from the farm?" he questioned. "I can remember going to my father once with my monthly paycheck and telling him, 'Dad, I added up the number of hours I've worked and divided that into what you paid me, and it looks like you're paying me only about seventeen and a half cents an hour.'"

There were some chuckles from the crowd, many of whom could relate to that statement. Steve finished the story. "My Dad thought it was the funniest thing he'd ever heard in his life. He laughed for a couple minutes, then looked at me with this serious look on his face and said, 'Son, I didn't realize I was overpaying you—*you're fired!*'" The place exploded in laughter.

Then Steve's tone changed. He told of how alcoholism, and the failure to pursue a professional baseball career, had brought him to the brink of suicide.

"It was April 15, 1991, when I woke up and said, 'Steve, you need to do one of two things. Throw a knife in your chest and get it over with, or get some help.'"

He went on to explain, "I didn't have the guts to kill myself, so I chose to get help. As God would have it, there was a pastor who led me to the book of John in the Bible, where I learned the truth about Jesus.

"In September, somebody put a copy of Billy Graham's *How to Be Born Again* on my coffee table. In that book Billy said that you could be sure of your place in heaven when you died. That was news to me. I thought that, when you died, if your good outweighed your bad you went to Green Bay—and if you were bad you went to Dallas!" he chuckled.

He added scripture to back up Billy's claim. "In Ephesians 2: 8-9 it says, 'For ye are saved by grace, through faith, not of works, it is a gift of God, lest any man should boast.' You can't earn heaven; it's a free gift received by choice, to trust Christ as your Savior and Lord.

"On October 1, 1991, I had a heart transplant. Oh no, not a physical one, but a spiritual one. On that day I asked Jesus Christ to come into my heart and life—and I have not been the same since. With God's help, I have been delivered from alcoholism, nicotine, gambling, and a few other things that had gripped me."

There weren't many dry eyes by this time. The night had arrived at the place the Holy Spirit had wanted it to go. I could tell. I could feel the extra heaviness of Steve's heart because of the news about Ken Ruettgers' retirement. I knew he'd make some special mention of it, but I didn't know just how powerfully Ken's decision would be woven into Steve's message this night. After a few stories about the faith of the men on the team and a few stories of Steve's relationships with them, he went in for the rescue.

"You know," he said, "tonight there are going to be members of the media who are going to tell you what a great left tackle Ken

Ruettgers was. And they'd be right. But you know, there is something they have not been privy to, that I have. There is something I can tell you that will reveal where this man is really coming from, something I'm sure you have never heard before."

The audience was glued to Steve's every word. He had given me no indication of what he was going to say about Ken that night. He boldly plunged ahead with the message God had asked him to deliver.

"You see, I know that for the last couple of years, Ken Ruettgers has exchanged his autograph for the answer to a question. People would approach him and ask, 'Ken, can we get an autograph?' Without hesitation he would reply, 'Sure, but may I ask you a question?' Standing with paper in hand, he would look at the person and ask, 'If you were to die tonight, and stand before God and He were to ask you, "Why should I let you into My heaven?" what would you say?'"

There was dead silence throughout the gymnasium.

"You see," said Steve, "In a hundred years from now is it gonna make a difference to you whether we won the Super Bowl?"

The crowd shook their heads from side to side, indicating that it wouldn't

"All that's gonna matter is where you are," he said with his voice trailing. He stared at them for about five seconds.

With the obvious guidance of the Holy Spirit, and in the words of his retired role model, Steve asked all in attendance that night the most important question in the world. "If *you* were to die tonight and stand before God and He were to ask you 'Why should I let you into My heaven?' what would you say?"

With a lump the size of a softball in his throat, Steve concluded, "The Bible says the answer to the question is that you have placed your trust in Jesus Christ as your Savior. All I know is that I used to drink two cases of beer a week. I don't do that anymore. I used to smoke a carton of cigarettes a week, but I don't do that anymore. This is just the beginning of what God has done for me. And he wants to do it for you, too," he said softly.

To make a long story longer, but with a happy ending, about twenty adults and children prayed to accept Christ as their Savior that night. Steve asked Pastor Naugle and me to join him on the floor as we prayed for those who wanted the free gift of God's salvation.

Steve Rose's friend Bob Gardinier.

It was snowing heavily as I drove the two of us home. We both were drained from the day and the huge blessing.

"I can't wait to tell Ken how the timing of his retirement announcement helped to usher some more people into the kingdom," Steve said excitedly. After about two minutes of silent reflection, Steve reached over and slapped me on my right shoulder. "Bob!" he shouted, as if a light had gone on. "Remember in church Sunday when Pastor told the congregation we needed to pray that my book would save souls?"

I replied, "Yeah!" And then I received a revelation from the Lord. "And you know, Pittsville is the geographical center of Wisconsin. It's just like in Act 1:8!"

Now it all made sense!

Two hours after we left Pittsville, we were back in the Fox Cities. A night that started out as "pittsville" ended up being a great night for many people *in* Pittsville. As Steve might ask, was it coincidence or God-incidence? And now that you've traveled with me through the Pittsville experience via the pages of this chapter, I'm certain that you have the right answer.

Author's note: Bob Gardinier, 37, has been a longtime friend and radio associate of Steve Rose. Bob is the Director of Network Development and Producer of the "Timeout" radio program for the Winners Success Radio Network.

The velvet-voiced Gardinier can be heard during the program along with co-hosts John Michels and Steve Rose.

Bob, his wife Linda, and their son Andy live in Appleton, Wisconsin.

Chapter 19

The Farmboy
and the Football Player

I peeled out of the Stadium View parking lot. I had just done a radio show on Friday, September 13, 1996, with Doug Kauffman and Bill Jartz over the noon hour on WDUZ in Green Bay. I was hoping I could catch a friend at his office. I pulled into the Packer parking lot and motioned to one of the guys that I had a book for him. I signed it. He shook my hand and thanked me. It was Santana Dotson.

Within minutes, head trainer and perennial great talk show guest Pepper Burruss was leading me into the Green Bay Packer training room.

There he was sitting on the training table receiving some sort of treatment for his bad knee that he was rehabilitating.

"Steve, what's cooking, man?" asked Ken Ruettgers. He was surprised to see me.

"Just wanted to bring you a copy of our 'best-selling-book-to-be,'" I quipped.

He paged through it as we chatted. Keith McKenzie looked over from one of the tables and said, "Hi!" Pepper was gathering some equipment around him when I couldn't help but remember one of Burruss' all-time great quotes from the show.

"Pep, that was a classic line, the second time you were on "Timeout," when you said, 'It's a shame you guys had to resort to having a trainer on.' Man, that was funny!" He smiled.

Kenny was very noncommittal when I asked him how his knee was coming along. He really had no clue back then if he was going to be able to play again. He was weeks away from even trying.

"Can I get some of the guys some books?" I asked the lineman.

"Let's go and put some in their lockers."

I was soon seated at a table in the locker room signing books. Ken went in for a shower. The rest of the guys had knocked off for the day. There were only a few left in the locker room at about 2:30. Maybe half a dozen.

Gilbert Brown ambled past. I knew he was big, but you have to see this guy close up to really appreciate what a load he is.

"Gilbert, how you doing?"

"Good," he said with a grin, toweling off his back.

Then I spotted another good friend over my left shoulder. It was George Koonce, one of the most polite people you'd ever want to meet, and a great guest, too. I sat next to him at his locker as we talked.

"Maybe I'll get some of these to send to my friends back home," he said as he spotted the page with the interview Kenny and I did with him.

I made my way back to the table. Gilbert had joined Earl Dotson and Gary Brown as they played a game of cards. There were Edgar Bennett and William Henderson pulling on shirts. Edgar's smile is even brighter in person than on TV! I heard a familiar voice from a man walking behind me. I didn't look around fast enough to see him. It was Mike Holmgren, asking Darius Holland a question.

I said hello to Darius and showed him the part in the book about him. He got a charge out of it. I set down books on Brett Favre's tennis shoes, Reggie's stuff, and then in Sean Jones' locker. At the risk of sounding like a gossip, I gotta tell you I have never seen a pair of flipflops as big as Jones'. Those things were skis!

Ken returned and he and I took the book for Coach Holmgren and put it in a cabinet where Ken said "He would be sure to find it." We walked into the room where they had all kinds of sweats, helmets, and other equipment.

We exchanged goodbyes in the parking lot and then we left. That was the last time I saw Kenny until we had an unplanned reunion for a "Timeout" show on October 21. As I recall that night, I must say that I really thought, by the gleam in Ken's eyes, that he was going to be able to pull it off and play last season. Of course I was wrong.

What will remain ingrained on my mind forever were Ken's kind words as we parted in the parking lot. "Hey, I'm proud of you!" he told me. You don't know what that meant to me. Neither did he. He's had his own book, and tons of success as a player, and I could tell how sincere he was. If I said he hadn't been on the top of my list of people I wanted to impress, after my family, I'd be fibbing. My wheels never touched the ground as I drove home that night.

Months later when we got together again, I'd had plenty of time to grieve the passing of my friend's football career. Except for an occasional phone call, I respected Ken's privacy as he let the idea of a new life take hold. Besides, I'm kind of speechless when it comes to trying to help others through mourning periods. I really didn't know what to say many times, so I just left the Ruettgers' alone. I figured their phone had been ringing enough. But now, it was time to get together.

The big man had told me he'd give me some stuff for my next book. So on a hot June morning in 1997, I grabbed the phone to call Ruettgers. We'd been playing phone tag for about three weeks. Because of my wild schedule with the book tour, we were never able to connect. Although Ken was retired from pro football, his life was far from empty. I dialed him up.

"Hello," he answered.

"Kenny, how's it going?"

"Great, what's up?" he asked.

"When can we get together for lunch?"

"How about today?"

"What time?"

"Eleven-thirty?"

"How about Red Lobster?"

"Let's do it," finished the retired lineman.

As I rolled up Highway 41, my mind drifted back to last November when Bob Gardinier and I were caught off guard in Pittsville by the news that Ken had retired. I couldn't help but reflect on the permanent impact this announcement had to both Ken's and my ministry. I'm telling you, God works in the most mysterious ways.

I recalled that it took me about a week before it really sunk in that it was over. What did "it's over" mean to Steve Rose? It meant no more watching my friend stand to Brett Favre's immediate left in the huddle, leaning in to hear the play. No more watching him arise after a play to adjust his knee brace.

It meant no more of hearing my wife say, "There's Ken!" when she'd see him on the field. It was a pretty selfish thing, really, for me to be hurt because it had all come to an end. And now, months later, after the dust had settled, it was business—er, fun and food—as usual for us.

I was pulling some books out of my trunk when I saw the Chevy Suburban of salvation pulling into the restaurant parking lot on the Lombardi Access Road in Green Bay. Ken smiled and pointed at me as he breezed by to find a parking space. I waved back.

He lumbered towards me as he had so many times in the WORQ studios where we'd done the "Timeout" show since 1994. He shook my hand. I couldn't get over how good he looked. He'd been taking great care of himself, obviously. It appeared my body was the only one that was retaining what Ken and I know as nature's greatest food—ice cream.

"Hey, you got an extra book for a friend of mine?" Ken asked respectfully. As an author himself, he knows that books don't grow on trees. They're just *made* from trees.

"Here's a hardcover for you and a softcover for your friend," I told him.

I asked who he wanted it signed to as we walked towards the entrance to our favorite eatery.

It wasn't until this meeting that I was able to ask Ken just how much pain he was in before he decided he couldn't take any more.

"When I came out of the tunnel for the Dallas Monday night game, I was going like, 'Why am I doing this?' It was just survival making every play," he confessed.

Kenny had told me that the pain was comparable to the most horrible toothache from his waist to his ankle. Just unbearable, but he tried so hard. He knew this was going to be the year. But he has standards, and if he could play up to them, he wasn't going to pull the team down. That's why he'd chosen to step away from the game seven months prior to our meeting.

The waitress made her way over and brought me a coke and the big fella a glass of water.

"Separate checks, guys?" she inquired.

"No, no, I'll take it," I said. "My friend quit his job last year and . . ." I smiled at Kenny and we burst out laughing.

Then we both flashed back to when I used to tease Ken during the show. "You know, if you had more than part-time, seasonal work, Sheryl [his wife] never would have had to do those Sentry commercials." She did some fantastic radio spots back in 1994. Ken always got a bang out of that. More than once, I asked the listeners to bring their job offers to him!

We ordered our usuals, Ken the blackened salmon, me the perch. Kenny ordered his salad dry, and passed on the crab legs he'd normally dip in butter.

"What are you gonna do?" I asked, hoping not to appear to be prying.

"Everyone has told me to not make any decisions for six months," he said. "Right now, I'm trying to find my significance outside of football."

He didn't mean his self-esteem was injured, but he was praying and seeking the Lord's guidance for his next move. Personally, I was thinking of a book tour he could join! I could see him signing copies of his book, *Home Field Advantage: A Dad's Guide to the Power of Role Modeling*, and my books.

Here's a man who could do anything—TV, radio, you name it. But you can be assured that any move Ken Ruettgers makes will be well considered and taken only after thoughtful prayer, and it will have the best interests and feelings of his family in mind.

In conversation, Ken did confirm that he'd been approached by certain political types about running for office. The thought of travel seemed to cause problems for him, but I don't think he'd be right for a political career, really.

We all know that to be involved in politics successfully means compromising. I don't think that's Ken Ruettgers. In God's word there isn't room for compromise, and that's his policy for life.

As we were eating he told me of the "Night in Wisconsin" he and John Michels took along with their wives. I knew right then, it was gonna be perfect for a chapter for this book (Chapter 11).

Ken thanked me as I picked up the check. Ken decided to order some decaf coffee. I joined him.

"You know, you used to joke about my job being part-time, and now I am totally unemployed." Somehow, I get the feeling old Ken wouldn't necessarily qualify for the food stamp program.

There was one time I began to wonder whether he was hurting for a couple pennies. That was in 1995. The postman brought a letter from Ken with postage due. Ken had put only a three-cent stamp on the letter! I called him later and told him, "Look, brother, if you need money for postage or groceries, just call." You know, now that I think of it, he still owes us twenty-nine cents. (Maybe this will scare it out of him)

Our time was finished. I joked that we hadn't even had time for our greatest passion—ice cream! I knew he must have been in a hurry. He had told Sheryl he'd be home by two. In the parking lot, I gave him a tape of one of my appearances. "Call me if you need me," were his last words to me that day.

He did call me a few days after hearing the tape. He enjoyed it. He also agreed to write this book's foreword.

As I drove home, I couldn't help remembering once again the hurt I felt when Ken retired. I recalled weeping one day to a point where I nearly had to pull over while driving. I can't describe what it felt like. For a man I have only spent probably a hundred hours with, I have really grown to love him.

I also thought about the poem. Yeah, I wrote and faxed him a poem right in the midst of the tough time. I didn't have the guts to call him. I was really afraid that it would be too painful for him, and me, well I thought I'd lose it for sure I nearly did, months later when he acknowledged it.

"Steve, I can tell you put a lot into that." The little boy in me felt good that he'd recognized it. I had put a good share of my heart down on paper. I'm not a poet, but here is what I faxed Ken just a couple weeks after the numbness had worn off for all of us.

I Just Thought You Should Know

By Steve Rose for Ken Ruettgers

The moment we met and did the first show . . . my life has
   never been the same. I just thought you should know
Your encouragement, words, and broad shadow have lent
   strength to my ministry for Christ. I just thought you
   should know.
Watching you persevere and be who you are despite who you
   could be astounds me. I just thought you should know.
Your discipline of a champion drips from you everytime I see,
   hear, or am with you. I just thought you should know.
Your talent is pale to the warmth of your heart, and your witness
   challenges me everyday. I just thought you should know.
You, Sheryl, and your wonderful family are a model of all a
   family should be and I love you all. I just thought you
   should know.
I can't wait to watch what God is going to do now for you.
   I pray to be a part of it. Just thought you should know.
You order the blackened salmon and I'll have the perch. I'm
   coming to take you there. I just thought you should know.
The Dairy Queens and Ben & Jerry's are excited to know they
   will see us more. I just thought you should know.
Our times together, away from the microphone, have been
   great blessings for me. I just thought you should know.
I pledge to be there for you always. I hope God can use our
   ministries again. I just thought you should know.
I have spent this time letting you know these many things on
   my hurting heart . . . Ken. I just thought you should know.
I can think of nothing greater than after *our* days, spending
   eternity in heaven with you. I just thought you should know.

For the first time since I've known Ken Ruettgers, I will make this confession to you. The day I met Ken, I thought I was going to meet a much different man. The press had convinced me that Ken was kind of a difficult guy, hard to get along with. I bought it. Well, right now I would like to apologize to Ken for believing that stuff.

It makes sense now. Ken, many didn't like you because of your conservative stance for the Lord. Why couldn't I figure it out that the light and the darkness will never see eye to eye? Forgive me. Why didn't I see that? I actually thought the morning I met Ken that he may be tough to work with. Wow! What a laugh that has turned out to be! That first morning, in September of 1994, two minutes into our meeting he knocked me off my chair.

"Steve, what kind of coffee and donut do you want me to bring you every week?" he asked me. He'd come to serve and not be served, just as Christ would. In fact, all the Christian Packers do. I'd had this idea that I'd be following these multi-millionaires around like a little puppy, catering to their every whim. What a joke that thought was. Ken, and those players like him are just normal guys

I told Ken many times before the shows, and especially during the writing of my two books, "Kenny, I'm gonna ruin your bad reputation." He'd chuckle, but I was serious.

And so here goes. For the record, Ken Ruettgers is a six-foot-six, 270-pound teddy bear. He's a man who will cry at the injustice of a life mistreated. He's a man who hurt deeply when others, including his teammates and coaches, thought he wasn't giving his best. God, you, and I knew he was . . . and always will.

Pardon me, if you feel I'm making a little to much of a man who silently played left tackle for the Green Bay Packers for eleven and a half years. But the fans made a fuss over him, too. It was during the off-season when we heard rumors that maybe the Packers weren't going to give him a Super Bowl ring. I loved the way you fans burned up the fax machine at the Packer offices. God bless you. I know Ken was overwhelmed. He told me he never felt claim to one.

Did you want him to have only one claim to greatness, that of being one of the greatest offensive linemen ever to don a Packer uniform? I don't think so. I'll bet you admire Ken Ruettgers because you learned to appreciate the more complete man he had become, and you learned about the many lives he's touched, including yours. Right? That's what I thought.

I suggest that if you ever have the opportunity to be around this lovable man of God, do everything you can to grab the opportunity. Be sure to get a hug or a handshake from this gentle man. And if you ever want to make him smile . . . just mention anything about Ben & Jerry's ice cream or the Dairy Queen. That'll do it.

Chapter 20

Diary of the Leap of Faith "Temporary Insanity" Book Tour

July 18, 1996
39 days to book release date
Green Bay, Wisconsin

Insanity requires preparation. It also has an origination. For many of you it maybe started with conception. For *Leap of Faith: God Must Be A Packer Fan*, it started with a reception, hosted by a receiver/music artist and a farmboy/author.

Robert Brooks and I invited the media from all over Wisconsin to join us for the announcement of the upcoming release of Robert's CD, called "Jump," and my book. Robert's CD would debut August 1, and the book a month later.

About 9:45 in the morning, I arrived with Chuck Towns, from WORQ, to get prepared for the eleven o'clock press conference. Jerry and the folks from Stadium View in Green Bay had everything ready to go. The impressive four-by-six-foot mural of the front cover was awesome as it was attached to the wall behind the podium.

Kim and Mom arrived shortly after and placed themselves in the front row. Jerry Ninneman, from my hometown *Campbellsport News*, was there with Campbellsport School Board president Bill Marchant. They had a few quick pictures taken with Adam Timmerman. Adam, a fellow farm boy, and his wife Jana had graciously come to support Robert and me.

At ten o'clock, the media started filling the joint. TV cameras stood on tripods and radio cassettes were piled on the head table. About five microphones were set on the podium where Brooks and I were to talk.

Also present was John Gillespe, who co-founded Rawhide Boys Ranch with Bart Starr. There was Greg Jensen, a former Packer, now with the Fellowship of Christian Athletes, in Madison. Green Bay Christian School principal Kurt Partain, who has since come to be a good friend, supported me that day.

My editor Larry Names was there, but remained inconspicuous. He wanted me to have the spotlight. He's that kind of a guy. He was the one who had straightened out the syntax and made my manuscript make sense.

About 10:45, Robert showed up dressed to kill in a brown satin outfit and brown sandals. I shook his hand and hugged him. We planned the strategy. Wayne Pankratz, one of my seventh-grade teachers from Campellsport, would introduce me, I would do an intro, then turn things over to Robert.

The forty-five-minute conference came off without a hitch. It was powerful. The media listened attentively to both our messages. They listened as Robert played the song, and as I told of my forthcoming book, telling how God's hand is in, on, and around this team.

Afterward, the media mobbed Robert and a couple radio stations sought me out. They shot some photos of Robert and me standing by the mural. As I was standing there, trying to be totally cool, Robert did the old "rabbit ears" thing to me. I was wondering why everyone was laughing.

Pat Breeden, from Mount Washington, Kentucky, who I talked about in Chapter 13, took some pictures and video. His parents Ruth and Jim were there, too.

"Man, this is gonna be great!" Robert would say, turning around and staring at the picture.

It was a rush to watch parts of the historic event from the day on Green Bay and Milwaukee TV news that night. It would turn out to

Steve Rose and his mother, Jean, ready for the Tampa Bay game and the start to the Leap of Faith *book tour.*

be a tough night to make news because that was the night nearby Oakfield got hit by a devastating tornado.

"I can't wait until September 1," was all that would go through my mind for the next 39 days. The *Leap of Faith: God Must Be A Packer Fan* tour had been launched. And it would be the greatest form of temporary insanity I could have ever have asked for.

Day 1
September 1, 1996
Tampa, Florida

Kim, Mom, Aunt Joyce, and I were beaming as we headed for the airport and our early morning flight to Tampa, where the Packers were to play the Buccaneers. I'd been waiting for the kickoff of the *Leap of Faith: God Must Be A Packer Fan* book tour for a long time.

Sunshine greeted our first signing on Sunday. I'd appeared along with Packer legend Ray Nitschke on behalf of America's Pack, the official fan club of the Green Bay Packers. Renowned artist Andy Goralski was with us because Ray was signing a print Andy had created.

What a thrill to sign the first of 40,000 books that would be sold over the next six months. It eased the pain of a nasty sunburn I'd gotten as Kim and I cooked ourselves on a beach in Clearwater the day before.

We got soaked in a rainstorm and looked like drowned rats by the time we made it into the stadium. The game was pretty anticlimactic. When Robert got knocked out, I got pretty nervous. After all, he and I were scheduled to "do Fond du Lac" in a couple weeks.

That night, after the game, we met the Roths from West Bend. Aunt Joyce told them, "My nephew is going to have a best-selling book!"

I could tell by the looks on their faces, they were thinking, "Yeah, sure." You know, I would have felt the same way. I could tell that they had no clue as to what we had with this book. Neither did we.

On Monday morning as we flew home, knowing that the tour was under way seemed to make my sunburn less painful. I thought to myself, "Aunt Joyce, I think you may be right, I think, we may have something here."

Day 7
September 7, 1996
Milwaukee, Wisconsin

After months of preparation and anticipation, the day had arrived for our first book signing in Wisconsin. It was on behalf of WVCY and the WVCY Bookstore. Earlier in the week, my boss, Vic Eliason, from the VCY America Network, had invited me to appear on WVCY-FM's syndicated national show called "Crosstalk." Vic is a mentor, the greatest non-compromising Christian I know.

On the show, we talked about the book and how God has chosen to use a group of individuals, who just happen to play football in Green Bay, for His purposes. During the show we promoted the book signing.

The sun was shining on this beautiful Saturday morning. I stopped at McDonalds to grab a cup of coffee, and hit the road. The trip took me about an hour and twenty minutes from Neenah to the WVCY Bookstore on Capitol Drive in Milwaukee.

Jim Schneider from the radio station and Steve Smith, from the store, greeted me when I arrived. I understood that you never know what can happen at these book signings. We were to sign books from 10 A.M. until noon. As it turned out, we weren't disappointed.

It started out kind of slowly, and then, wow, it really picked up. We had people ten to fifteen deep at times. We had a nice display of pictures of me and many of the Packers who had been on the show over the years. The kids really liked those.

My editor Larry Names showed up with some more books. We went through about a hundred books. It was actually a "zoo" for a while, but I just assumed this was normal.

I did about sixty bookstores during the nine-month run, and never have we come close to this first success. WVCY is a non-compromising Christian station. Was it coincidence or God-incidence that the biggest signing we've ever done was at their bookstore and promoted through their network? You tell me.

Day 63
November 2, 1996
Green Bay, Wisconsin

Mark Ellis phoned me around the middle of October to ask me if I'd like to join him for a "live" remote WVBO-Radio was doing from the Bay City Chrysler dealership in Green Bay. I'd do a signing and appear with a few of the Packers.

With my editor Larry Names' help, we were there and set up by 12:30. Mark, who is quite the radio personality, was doing live radio breaks inviting Packer fans to come out and have some free brats, popcorn, and fun. There was also the possibility that they might buy a car or two.

Packer players Shannon Clavelle and Keith McKenzie stirred the crowd as they arrived about one o'clock. Sean Jones drew lots of attention as he lumbered in the back door fifteen minutes later.

"Sean, did you get my copy of the book I put in your locker a couple weeks ago?" I asked curiously.

"Yeah, it was good." I had Sean sign a couple of books for me.

At about three o'clock, a slightly-built guy joined the others in autographing whatever items were put in front of them.

"Who's that?" I recall asking Mark.

"I'm not sure. You know, you take the numbers off these guys and you can't always tell who's who, right?" said Ellis.

"Tell me about it. I never know until Ken introduces them to me," I admitted.

Top picture: Steve visits with Chuck and Carole Kirsop, of Milwaukee.
Bottom picture: Robert Brooks with David Rose, Steve's father.

I joked with the "new" man there. I couldn't get over how small he was—small for a football player, that is. "Must be a defensive back," I thought.

Later, as I was about to leave, I felt no real need or reason to get his autograph. After all, he was one of the unknowns back then. His name was Desmond someone—yeah, Desmond Howard!

Day 69
November 8, 1996
Wausau, Wisconsin

I was running on fumes. It felt like my eyelids were being held open with toothpicks. I had gotten home from West Bend at eleven o'clock the night before, and now it was 4:30 the following morning.

I was on my way to Wausau for a 6:45 appearance on WSAW TV-7. After the TV, it would be radio interviews, and then a signing with former Packer Brian Noble at his Pro Image store there.

I met Bill Cooper in the Denny's parking lot in Rothschild at 6:30. Bill is the general manager and partner in Brian Noble's enterprise.

Upon arrival at the TV station, I was introduced to Bobbie Brooks, a pretty, talented young lady who hosts the "7 in the Morning Show" along with Jeff Thelen. He's a fellow graduate of Campbellsport High School!

We spent the rest of the day doing radio and did WAOW TV-9 News before heading for the signing at Pro Image. It went great.

As Noble signed books with me he said, "Look at this." People were about fifteen to twenty deep, which isn't bad even for Tom Clancy, I guess. "This guy isn't even a football player and still has people lined up out into the hall!" said Noble.

"Brian," I loved what I read in the *Journal Sentinel* the other day when you said that nothing comes before your relationship with Christ," I told him as we signed.

Later, Noble bought ribs at Tony Roma's. I for one, was glad that the tide of blessing had turned to me from him for a change.

Days 72-75
November 11-14, 1996
Louisville, Kentucky

I really wasn't sure why I was on an airplane going to Louisville, Kentucky. I did feel that the Lord had a hand in it, however. The

Breedens picked me up at the airport and graciously put me up for four nights.

The morning after our arrival, I appeared with Kevin McKnight on Louisville's version of the 700 Club. It was great! A Cowboy fan and a Packer fan on the same program.

"My brothers in the Lord precede any allegiance to a football team," said McKnight. That made me feel better. From there I went to WJIE-Radio, located in the same studios, for an interview.

I walked the halls of Evangel Christian School. It was there that I felt God calling me to speak in Christian schools. I have done so ever since.

On Tuesday night we went to Damon's, ate ribs, and watched the filming of the Paul Hornung show. Pete Rose was the guest. I got a few shots with Pete and me together—a pair of Roses. I posed with Hornung, too.

"Yeah, Jim Breeden gave me a copy of your book," he told me. I had him sign one for Kim, who had to stay home and work. (Somebody has to.)

By Thursday afternoon, I was on WHAS with Terry Meiners, the most popular radio man in those parts. He is also a diehard Packer fan,

Steve signs a copy of Leap of Faith *for a young Packer fan.*

which aliens consider to be a sign of intelligence on earth. We gave a way some books and promoted the book signing that night at the Hawley-Cooke Bookstore.

At six o'clock I arrived for the signing. Fans were lined up and decked out in green and gold. I couldn't believe it—the further away you get from Green Bay the crazier this Packermania thing is. It was nuts with Packer fans that evening.

Before I left the store, the owner said, "Be sure to come back when the sequel is out!" He told us we outsold some TV network guy who had been in a week before. A great trip . . . just great.

Day 98
December 7, 1996
Madison/Delafield, Wisconsin

At five o'clock in the morning I was at the Express Convenience store borrowing some energy in a coffee cup. It was two hours to Madison for a 7:45 interview with Dan Smith on WISC TV-3 in "Madtown." I pulled in there at 7:15. I was escorted to the set and miked.

As we were doing this bit during the show, the news guy comes crashing onto the set to bring us some coffee. It was great! I answered all the usual questions. Nice people.

"Can I get a copy of the tape?" I inquired after it was over. "Mom and Dad always like to see this stuff."

I cut out for breakfast and then by eleven o'clock I was signing books at the Family Bookstore in the East Towne Mall. Months earlier, Renee had asked me to come. It went well. The highlight was meeting Vicki Myers' parents, Stan and Patricia Hazard. Vicki is Pastor Myers' wife.

By two o'clock, we were across town at Barnes & Noble. It was there, after we signed about forty books, that Sherry Klinkner gave me the idea to use a Brooks continuation picture for this book—the very picture you see on the front cover of this book!—as a way of forming a continuity between the two publications.

By four, I was going *way* too fast to the Little Professor in Delafield, at least seventy miles away. I made it in record time.

"I wish I could stay, but I'm on my way to church," said the first lady in line there. That kind, warm lady turned out to be none other than Donna Morgan, a sister in the Lord, a Packerwomaniac, and a family therapist who contributed to this book.

That was quite a day. I was given a great suggestion and some new friends. I think it was this day that God told me to be alert for *who* He would bring into my path along the way. I realized, like Reggie with football, my book was the platform for meeting people.

Day 109
December 19, 1996
Beloit, Wisconsin

In November my phone rang. "Steve, this is Mike Staub, from Rock County Christian in Beloit. We'd love to have you come down and talk to the kids," he said.

"I'd love to come down." Mike explained that they had nothing to offer for expenses or an honorarium. I hesitated and gave it some thought. Then, I knew the right thing to do. "Mike, you can't write a book called *Leap of Faith* without taking one every once in a while. I feel the Lord telling me to come. He'll provide."

I was there in the morning for eight o'clock chapel to speak to the kids. Mike Staub led me to the gym. Very ordinary, humble kids; I thought they were pretty receptive to my message. They gave me a nice round of applause. My hat and chest sizes were swelling a bit.

Then came one of the most uncomfortable things I ever experienced on the book tour. Mike Staub turned his body toward me but still faced the kids.

"Steve came here on a leap of faith, you guys. But Steve," he said turning his gaze toward me, "We've decided to take up a love offering for you."

I just about sank into the floor. Good Lord, I was moved. What love. I could do one of three things. Jump up and yell no. Go out in the hall and cry, or semi-weep and take it. I chose the latter.

Imagine 14-year-olds pulling money out of their pockets for you. Good Lord, I was moved. Tears fell.

A girl named Elizabeth came up to me after and gave me a hug. That was it . . . I lost it. I clutched her neck and cried. I'll never forget the humility the Lord showed me there. The day I learned it pays even better—when you take a leap of faith.

Day 157
February 5, 1997
Hartland, Wisconsin

I punched the button on my answering machine and heard, "Steve, Sue and I would like to take you out to lunch after you speak at the school." I called my friends from my hometown to confirm.

The caller's kids go to Country Christian School in Nashotah. Have you ever been to Nashotah? Even among the Wisconsin folks, I bet there are only a few who have had the treat. Technically, I think Country Christian School is in Hartland. There, that clears it up, doesn't it? Anyway, it's just west of Milwaukee.

The invitation had come from Bob Pereirra of the school and my friends were graciously following up with the invitation to make lunch a part of the day.

As usual, I couldn't wait. I have so much to share with kids in all schools, but especially the Christian schools.

I poured my heart out to two groups of students there. All the while, I thanked God for two friends from home who chose to come and support me.

Afterwards, Sue took a picture of me and the man all of us from Eden have come to become so proud of. He's a man who will never forget where he came from. A man who is a walking testimony of what a life surrendered to Christ can do for the kingdom—and the game of baseball.

At 11:30, my friends and I were seated at the Picnic Basket to grab a bite to eat, get caught up on the news, and just to enjoy our fellowship. It was a very special hour for me. My friends ate tacos and I had pizza. I am so moved by the love for the Lord these two people have. Their hearts are so soft. What a blessing to spend time with my friend, Jim Gantner, of the Milwaukee Brewers, and his wife, Sue, the day the *Leap of Faith* "TI" Book Tour stopped in Nashotah.

Day 187
March 7, 1997
West Bend, Wisconsin

Last December, Mark Fector from Lighthouse Ministries in West Bend, Wisconsin, approached me with an invitation while I was signing books in the West Bend Pharmacy.

Every year, Mark and the people from Lighthouse Ministries put on a huge youth event called "Teen Breakaway." It's a powerful event attended by hundreds of kids.

"How'd you like to be our keynote speaker?"

"I'd be delighted. Just get the date and information to me."

The day of the event came quickly. I confess now that I was incredibly exhausted that night from the tour. I had concerns that I might not be at my sharpest.

Upon arrival, Mark Fector led me through a sound check as Vessels of Honor and Candles Amidst, two musical groups who would entertain that night, rehearsed.

The evening's events began at seven, and by 8:45 I was pumped and prepared to comfort and confront seven hundred youth! I got my chance.

As I poured my heart out for nearly an hour I felt a presense of the Holy Spirit moving upon me and over the entire room. At the Spirit's invitation, nearly sixty-five people chose to come forward to make a commitment to accept Jesus Christ as Lord and Savior.

As I left the stage, I immediately began to feel tired. God had given me strength while I spoke. I am amazed how God can give us the power to go on when our minds and bodies are week.

As I watched the video later with the Fectors and some folks from the event, all I could say was, "Those words were not mine, you guys." We all knew whose they were. The same One who provided the words for the book you're holding right now.

Day 209
March 29, 1997
Appleton, Wisconsin

This would turn out to be a very peculiar day, one with a unique experience I will not forget anytime soon. It included a wakeup call from the Lord through one of his servants.

"Gosh, I sure am important," I'd told a lot of my friends lately. Especially my wife. She hadn't caught on that best-selling authors shouldn't have to do menial housework. She wasn't buying it.

I wasn't starving for attention during this time and it was evidenced this day. At about 11:40 on my way to a gig, I was literally stopped in my car by someone on a street in Appleton. He leaned on my car window and began raving about my book, the radio show, and me.

"I just want you to know that I loved your book. I've been listening to your show with Ken for years. Keep up the good work." He wasn't finished. I took a deep breath in relief, thinking maybe I was on the verge of a move of mercy.

"So, here's your drivers license and here's your ticket for going forty miles and hour in a thirty-mile zone." He continued, "In order for me to be consistent and fair, I need to give you this." God's laws are consistent and fair, too, aren't they? After all, what's wrong with getting what we deserve?

What a unique experience! As the scripture points out in Galatians, "As you speed so also shall you get a ticket." (Or something like that)

As I was going to leave, he said, "Steve, my name is Mike and I'm a member of Cops for Christ." With that, I was glad that he had stopped me. Yeah, sure. But I was glad that he was helping to bring a dose of humility and reality to my life. It was time to slow down. As a reminder, I had a pink ticket and an appointment to pay a fine of $116.90.

I haven't felt quite as important, or been in such a hurry, ever since.

Day 235
April 24, 1997
Rockford, Illinois

I went to Rockford, Illinois, at the invitation of Pastor Denver Bittner to speak to a men's accountability group. As it turned out, there was an even higher calling for me to have been invited there, at least to a hurting man named Larry.

This group had enjoyed meeting Ken Ruettgers the year before. It was a tough act to follow. "I don't sing, dance, or play football," I told the group of about eighty guys. "And if you talk to my wife, she'll tell you I don't do much of anything," I joked.

As I spoke, I locked eyes with an African-American brother, who I could tell was moved by the message. I add, I am not the message, but only the messenger. I'm a nobody saved by Somebody.

Afterward, this man, who looked to be in his thirties, approached me and handed me a note. "Pray for me," he pleaded with a tear in the corner of his eye. I embraced him. I opened this stunning note later.

Dear Mr. Rose,

I came to this meeting because I was invited by Dr. Olson. I really enjoyed your talk. You came here for me. The Lord used you tonight to speak to me. I am a black man that loves the Lord, but I have struggled in drug addiction.

I am married to a very special saved woman who I have hurt so bad. I am supposed to be a minister, one of the world's best ministers.

I would buy a book, but I have only a dollar to my name. But, I don't want a book, I want Jesus. You've touched my life.

Larry

And I thought I had orchestrated my schedule. Apparently not. As I was reminded by Larry, it was clearly God who scheduled me into Rockford.

Day 256
May 15, 1997
Albany, Wisconsin

I could feel from the moment I heard the humble, serene voice of Pastor Bob Krell, from First Baptist Church in Albany, Wisconsin, that it was imperative I take him up on his invitation. Albany is just south of Madison.

"We'd really like to have you come here," he said.

"Bob, if you want me, you got me," I told him.

I called the pastor the night before from a motel in Sparta.

"I was wondering if you would come and visit a lady who is in the last stages of a battle with cancer?" he inquired. Word was she had two to three months to live. I told him I'd be pleased to stop in and meet and pray with her.

At two o'clock I spoke to the students at the high school. A great group of kids.

At four, we walked across the street from the school to the home of the woman Pastor had invited me to meet. There I was introduced to Linda. She looked to be in her forties. She was very weak, but in great spirits. Her medication was being fed intravenously as she lay on her bed.

"Linda, do you ever ask God . . . 'Why me?'"

"No, I ask him, 'Why not me?'"

I have never heard anything so sacrificially powerful as those words. She was ready to meet her Lord, Jesus. She has accepted Jesus Christ as her Savior. The Bible *promises* her a place in Heaven because of this decision (John 6:47). That's why she had no fear. It was obvious to me.

It was time to go. I gave her a book. She was a Packer fan. "I'll try to read it," she smiled.

"Linda, if I don't have the opportunity to see you again, I'll see you in Heaven," I whispered in her ear. I hugged her, kissed her cheek and left. As I walked out her door, I realized my problems weren't so bad. No . . . I realized I didn't have any problems at all.

Author's note: On July 17, 1997, Linda Lemaster died. She was ushered out of her physical suffering and went to be with the Lord. Pastor Kress presided over her memorial service at the First Baptist Church in Albany. Before she died, Linda wanted me to let you know that today, as she is in eternal rest, there is only one decision for her that matters. According to Linda and God's Word, it was the day she accepted Jesus Christ as her Lord and Savior. Is that a leap of faith you've taken yet? If not, why not today?

Day 295
June 30, 1997
Green Bay, Wisconsin

I pulled into a cozy Green Bay neighborhood with Jim Coursolle, a friend and renowned radio person. We approached a modest brick home and rang the doorbell.

Jim introduced me to the woman who answered the door. "It's nice to see you," she said. "I'm reading your book."

"Pleasure to meet you, ma'am," I said.

"I'm paying my property taxes," she said. "Excuse me, I want to make sure I haven't misplaced the bill." Jim and I wandered around and looked at the great photos on her wall. My book sat on a desk with a rubber band around it and a book mark stuck in the pages.

We sat in her quaint living room. This spry, effervescent woman had been a jet setter many years ago. She was a buyer for Prange's department store. She told of how men by the name of Lavvie Dilweg, Verne Lewellen, and Don Hutson had come over to visit with her and her husband so many years ago.

Steve visits with Marguerite Lambeau, the first *first lady of the Packers, in her home in Green Bay.*

Her husband was a coach. "My husband would wake up and write Xs and Os in the middle of the night," she laughed. "I'd turn over and he'd be writing."

Jim Coursolle asked her, "When we get to Heaven, will you introduce us to some of the guys who used to come here?"

"Sure," she answered.

"We are all going to Heaven, aren't we," asked Coursolle.

"I hope so," she said with hope in her eyes.

Maybe you've heard of this lady, and even her husband. She's 98 years young. Her name is Marguerite—Marguerite Lambeau, the first lady of the Green Bay Packers! Maybe you've heard of her husband, Curly, too. They named a stadium after him.

Chapter 21

Looking for a Leap of Faith

Robert Brooks and I were frustrated as we talked on the telephone. The topic of discussion was how we were going to provide a picture of the popular Packer doing his patented "Lambeau leap" for the front cover of my first book, *Leap of Faith: God Must Be A Packer Fan.* (If you're looking for a recommendation to read it just talk to my Mom, she really thought it was good. And if that's not enough talk to my Dad—he really liked it, too!)

That story was written from January through April of 1996. In May its pages were being typeset for publication. There was one huge problem. We still didn't have the front cover photo we wanted, the one that would capture the love affair between the Packer players and fans. It would certainly help me to plead my case that God was bringing his Christ-like love to the people in Green Bay. Just five months earlier, on December 22, 1995, my phone rang. It was my friend and mentor, Jim Zielinski, who suggested I write a book about what the Lord was doing in the inner circle of the Green Bay Packers. Jim, per usual, your suggestion, 40,000 books later, turned out to be a great one. But not before a few anxious moments.

Brooks and I couldn't believe that a five-month search could not turn up one snapshot of the "Leaper of the Pack" doing one of his trademark jumps. What would have been ideal would have been a picture of the receiver about three feet off the ground with outstretched arms, with his right side leading the way to the stands. Of course, the fans would be reaching out to him, too, in the emotion of it all. Brooks had done numerous leaps and we couldn't believe that all the photographers in all the universe hadn't provided one photo for us. How could it be that this image didn't exist?

"You just can't appreciate the angle you need to have," said one photographer. "You know, you really have to be there at the right time," another would tell me. What was most mysterious was that the picture I envisioned was really the first vision God put it my heart and mind when He called me to write the book. I was certain the vision was from the Lord—wasn't it?

I have to admit I really thought this picture would be one of the first things God would provide for this project. If my assumption was wrong, it could be fatal for the book. "But Lord, this picture in my mind is out there, isn't it?" I asked. "You wouldn't give me this inspiration and then not provide the tools, would You?"

But for some reason, the Lord had decided to throw me for a loss in the backfield.

In late May I thought I spotted an opening. I had found a perfect picture of Brooks jumping into the stands. However, it had been taken off of video. It was from a leap of Brooks' during the Falcons game in the 1995 playoffs.

"Robert, you won't believe it," I told him. "We have it!" Incidentally, Brooks was searching for a similar picture to put on the front cover of his CD single called "Jump."

"What did you find, man?"

I was really fired up as I told Brooks about the shot I'd found. "It's great, Robert. You are being shown from the back, there are a bunch of people reaching for you—including Santa Claus!" I remember how thrilled I was because I thought how neat it would be to tell people that not only is God a Packer fan, but so is Santa Claus, which must mean the Easter Bunny is, too! It was perfect.

There were two problems. One, the video belongs to the NFL, and cannot be used without special permission. Our legal counsel told us that there have been only two times that this has ever been allowed. Basically they said that the chance of being able to use the picture and avoid a lawsuit from the NFL was about the same as the average temperature being 75 degrees in December in Green Bay.

Honestly, if I had not known up until this point, beyond a shadow of a doubt, that God had written the book and it was He who had given me the vision for the front cover picture, I would have been frightened. I knew God's hand was in this too, and I took a leap of faith to continue to believe that God wouldn't provide the vision without also fulfilling it.

"But God, the publisher needs the picture, like soon!" I prayed.

Brooks and I prayed and plotted our next action. We thought maybe an artist's drawing of the picture was the answer. This way we could not legally infringe on anyone. There are a lot of great artists in Wisconsin who can make drawings look more real than actual pictures.

A few days after our last conversation in early June, Robert was coasting down U.S. Highway 41 on his way to watch the Chicago Bulls take on the Seattle Supersonics in the 1996 NBA Championship series. From his cellular phone, he called me.

"Steve, it's Robert. Got some great news!"

Boy, was I ever up for some good news.

He went on. "The Green Bay Packer Hall of Fame is going to be shooting a commercial in Lambeau Field next Friday and they want me to do a couple Lambeau leaps. They said they will let us use a picture for the front cover of the book and CD!" he exclaimed happily.

"Praise the Lord," I said.

Two weeks later I was pulling up to Robert's mailbox where he had left the slides of the commercial leap for me. He wasn't home because he had to catch a flight. I held them up to the sun and could see the one that would probably work the best.

After having it blown up, I realized that something was a tad different on the photos from the vision I'd had. Robert was being shot from his left side and back. But, I had seen him from the front in my mind. I wondered why. Then, within a couple days the Lord told me and I'll share it shortly.

The picture was there all the time, but sometimes God wants us to get down on our knees and bow our hearts before him and ask with an unwavering faith. Clearly in this case, God had it there all the time. I just needed to trust Him, and honestly, it wasn't easy.

If you take a look at the front cover of *Leap of Faith: God Must Be A Packer Fan*, as well as the front cover of this book, you'll see a couple telltale signs that these are not shots from a real game. The main one is the weather. It was 93 degrees when these shots of Brooks and Packer faithful were taken. Don't you think it would have been a good suggestion to put someone in a winter coat or something?

Still, I had the one burning question I brought up earlier. Why was the picture the Lord provided for the book a little different from the one I saw in my heart? Here's what He told me in my spirit.

"Steve, I will always have a little different twist than what you think. I hold your visions and dreams and will provide all that's necessary for you to fulfill them in accordance with My will." He wasn't kidding.

Friend, this is just one of the many miracles that were needed to bring you the first book, and this one as well. I share this miracle about the picture and other provisions to assure you that this book as well as the first is a miracle.

Were there any lessons in this calling for me? Yeah! The first is that when God calls any of us to do something He will equip us. He will provide what is needed—like He did with the picture He had put in my mind. And He wouldn't call me to bring a message to His people without providing it, but I had to trust Him one hundred percent. Trust and obey, for there is no other way.

Is there something you feel you are called upon to do today, yet you are having trouble taking the big leap of faith? Do it! All I can say is, just do it! There are miracles waiting around the corner. One of the greatest lies of the enemy, and He has many, is that you have to be Reggie White, Michael Jordan, or somebody super-special for God to provide a miracle. Do you need a miracle? Pray for it and ask God to work in accordance with His will.

Be prayerful and confident that God will provide not always what you want, but what you need. Beware, there may be some work involved, just as there was in getting our picture. However, God will make your Leap of Faith available for you, just when you need it, as He has for Robert and me when we were searching for *our* miracles.

Chapter 22

God Loves Packer Fans.
He Told Me So.

I had quite a startling dream the other night. As I slept, I felt myself floating through a long tunnel. It was like being on an escalator, only there was no gravity. It led me to a gate where an angel with green and gold wings met me. "I think you'll enjoy your brief stay here," the angel said.

"What do you mean, 'brief stay?'" I asked him. He offered no answer.

"Excuse me, but where am I?" He acted as if he had never even heard me.

The fluffy-winged one's next statement was, "You have been brought here to visit a very distinguished place, but only for a short time. Then, you must return and tell the others,"

"Tell them what?"

"You will know before you leave here," he smiled. I have never seen teeth that gleamed like his.

Without moving a step, in the blink of an eye, I found myself alone in a room. I can't explain it, but it felt as if I had vaulted ahead well into the future. A couple hundred years? A thousand? I wasn't sure, but I knew I had left a good share of time behind me.

The room was in what appeared to be some sort of palace. It was huge and everything was decorated in green and gold. It resembled some sort of Green Bay Packer Wax Museum. There were motionless Packer players all over the place.

Although there were no lights in this place, there was an intense but not blinding golden light that shone throughout the round and spacious domed chamber. I would guess the room was about fifty yards in diameter.

I wandered aimlessly, beginning to look at the guys. I recognized all of them. Suddenly, an older man's voice shouted out, about twenty feet behind me. He called, "Sir, come this way. I am your host." He looked so familiar. His balding head glowed, but there was some white hair on his head. He wore glasses. His voiced rang with authority. I was sure I had heard it before.

"Who are you, anyway?"

"My name is Lee. I am the curator here," he smiled.

"Who do you work for here?" I inquired.

"My boss, Vince, who works under the 'man upstairs,'" he answered proudly.

We talked Packers for a while and this guy knew everything! Larry McCarren's middle name, Tony Mandarich's shoe size, you ask him, he'd tell you.

I still really needed to know where I was. As I looked around, the green and gold, the familiar statues, I had an idea. "Lee, is this . . . ?"

"No . . . but you'll know in time before you have to go. You must move along and not waste time. Listen closely," he said. "Many will depend on what you tell them after you leave here. Will you be faithful to share the message you receive here when you get back? In a short time the gate will close once more behind you. But you will return someday and I will see you then."

Now I was really curious as to what was going on.

"Now, be on your way. When you have completed your initial visit with some friends on this floor, you'll need to visit with the 'man upstairs.'"

"Wait . . . wait . . . wait . . . ," I protested. "Who is the 'man upstairs?'"

"As I said, when you get to the end of your tour on this floor, you will see a narrow staircase. Take the steps till you get to the top. Now, son, really, I must go about my duties," he said.

"Now look, just where am I, anyway?" I pleaded one last time.

"Enjoy your stay with us," he replied as he began to vanish, totally ignoring my pleas. In seven to ten seconds he was a mist, then gone. Once again, I was alone.

The peaceful tones of a pipe organ began to play the prettiest music I have ever heard. I can't begin to describe it. I got the courage to begin walking. Something was strange. As I walked, I really couldn't feel my feet touching the soft, dry, dark green carpet.

I made my way towards the first wax figure. It was Bart Starr. He was proudly wearing his #15 jersey and that great smile of his. There was a letter there for me from the two-time Super Bowl MVP. It said, "Steve, be sure to tell everyone to look beyond Lambeau Field. Also, remind them that the greatest things can happen during the coldest times of life."

I got it! He was talking about the "Ice Bowl." It was colder than an IRS office when he scored that winning touchdown on New Year's Eve, 1967. I was sure that's what he meant as I read on.

"Tell everyone the path is narrow, much like the one I followed behind Jerry Kramer to score on the sneak to beat the Cowboys. Everyone has an invitation to the greatest end zone of all, but it's up to you to tell them how they can find it."

It was signed, "Gratefully, Bart Starr. P.S. Say Hi to John Gillespe for me when you get back."

What did he mean—when I get back?

As I proceeded, I recognized many other faces from the "Time-out" show. "Man, that must have been hundreds of years ago," I felt in my mind.

There was George Koonce. Back home he had told me how he stayed in shape by eating chicken. He still looked good. I remembered how great it was to visit with him in the locker room after my first book came out. Nice man. What a shame he didn't get to play in that Super Bowl against the Patriots.

Aw . . . there was Charles Jordan. What a nice man. What a great testimony. He went from watching people being shot on the streets of L.A. to a life changed through Jesus Christ. I recalled how sick I felt when the Packers let him go to the Dolphins. What was he doing in this room, anyway?

"Hey, it's Adam Timmerman," I yelled. If there was a man I could relate to during the "Timeout" show, it was him. A farmboy, Chevy commercials. Great haircut. He was still smiling.

It took me a couple of minutes to recognize Paul Coffman. It was the wavy hair. I remember Ken Ruettgers telling me how he had never seen a life changed more than Paul Coffman's when he came to Christ. Remember old number 82? Paul was one of Lynn Dickey's favorite targets at tight end, back in the '80s.

Speaking of the '80s, there was John Anderson. A wonderful man. He and Tom Pipenes, from Channel 6 in Milwaukee, were so gracious to me during my book tours. High School in Waukesha, college in Michigan, and then a career with the Packers. And now he was here in . . . well, I wasn't sure where he was. I didn't even know where I was, but I had an idea.

I found myself in front of Sean Jones. He looked as if he was still working out! What a physique. I recalled how moved Packer fans were way back in the 1996 season when he took a pay cut to help the Pack win the Super Bowl. A big guy, with a real big heart for his team.

There were other present, and some past, players in this intriguing place. Bryce Paup, Mark Ingram, Don Beebe, Keith Jackson, and Harry Galbreath.

On the far side of this magnificent room I found Johnny Holland, Guy McIntyre, LeShon Johnson, Darius Holland, Pepper Burruss, Kent Johnston, and John Michels. There was Coach Holmgren, too. Those were the only ones I could see. There were more.

Then I came upon two very special people. There he was. It was Reggie. He was wearing his Most Valuable Cheesehead T-shirt! Did he also have a message for me to take back? I was looking for it when suddenly I heard White's raspy voice—but his lips weren't moving! This voice was coming from the depths of the soul of the minister of defense.

"Steve, go and tell them about Jesus. The greatest thing about the people of Wisconsin is they aren't afraid of the Gospel, the good news of salvation through Christ. Go tell 'em, brother." He wasn't finished.

"Does the media finally believe God sent me to Green Bay to talk about Jesus? Or do they still think it was about winning a Super Bowl?"

Then he laughed for about five seconds till his voice became still and silent.

I turned to my right and walked towards the last two figures. A big smile came to my face as I recognized Robert Brooks. What a sweet man. It was he whom God chose to take His love into the stands at Lambeau Field. Brooks was probably the most lovable guy in the history of the Green Bay Packers. As I looked upon his wax figure I noticed he was still skinny. Leaning on his left foot was his CD single, "Jump."

Tears streamed down my face when I recognized the last man. It was my radio partner and friend, Ken Ruettgers. He was always a defender of the truth. His platform was football, but his passion was Jesus Christ, his family, and serving his fellow man. Pinned to Ruettger's shirt was a picture of his family. At his feet was a copy of his book, *Homefield Advantage: A Dad's Guide to the Power of Role Models*. It went back to 1995. There was an empty pint of Ben & Jerry's ice cream at his feet. That must have been why he had such a big smile on his face!

There was a small note for me in his left hand. It said, "Steve, when we get together, let's go to Red Lobster and the Dairy Queen."

But when was I going to be able to see him? All the guys talked about seeing me later. Where were they now? When would we have the chance to see each other again?

I reached my left arm around Ken's waist and pulled my head to his rib cage. Then, something extremely weird happened. In what can't be measured in any element of time, he and the rest of the guys disappeared! Poof, gone. The room was now empty.

I turned around and all that was left in the room was a staircase. It must have been the one I was instructed to take before I left.

With the initial part of my tour over, I cautiously made my way toward the steps. They were made of pure gold. The light beaming off the golden steps and railing was quite a sight! As the man said, the staircase was narrow. It was also winding and steep. There was a different scripture verse on each step.

As I got to the top of the stairs I spotted a single room. A sign on the door said, "Upper Room." The door opened for me. What I saw there will remain etched in my mind forever.

There He was . . . at least I thought I knew who He was! His face shone brightly. His skin was so clean and smooth. His eyes penetrated right through me. His embrace comforted me. I knew who this was, but why was I here to see Him?

He showed me to a chair. He sat upon what looked like a throne. He smiled lovingly as if He was happy to see me.

"My son, I have been expecting you. Before the world began, I made this appointment with you," He said. "Did you enjoy seeing your friends here? It's been a while since you have seen many of them."

"Yes . . . it has."

"Did you receive their messages to take with you?"

"I did," I answered. "Sir, why are the guys here? Where did they disappear to?" One more time, I had to see if I could discover just where I was.

"And, where am I, anyway?"

"Didn't you read My book?" he said without hesitation.

"You mean the Bible?"

"Is there any other?" He smiled. "And your friends, let's just say they are waiting for you, OK? They, like I, pray that you will carry the message back to the beloved Packer faithful all over the world. Matter of fact, they recommended you to Me. Ken Ruettgers and Robert Brooks said some pretty nice things about your ministry."

"So, anyway, it is official. I have chosen you to be My public relations spokesperson to link Packer fans, and all in the world who will listen to you proclaim My Gospel," He said, smiling at me.

"I'm flattered, but why am I here?"

"To tell people how to get to Heaven," He said bluntly. "Answer this, Steve. How do you think most people think you get there?"

"That's easy—by being good, right?"

"That's correct my son. You must take the truth back with you to all the world that the answer is in Me! Tell them My gift at Calvary for them is what I offer. It was necessary for Me to die there for their sins. But they must come as little children and admit they are sinners. Unless they are born again they shall not see the Kingdom" [John 3:3].

As He spoke, it was like a giant magnet attracted His words to my brain so I could not forget them. I froze before Him. Notes weren't necessary. His words would never leave my mind.

"You will be leaving in just a few moments, but first you must listen to more instructions. Hundreds of thousands of people back in Packerland *must* hear the things I am going to share with you."

Something crazy happened as He continued to talk. His words boomed like thunder and there was a resounding echo to them.

"Tell the Packer fans I love them! Reggie was right. I sent him there because I knew they would accept this message of salvation.

"It is in My love and mercy that I have chosen to meet them at Lambeau Field. Why do you think I sent so many good and faithful servants like Ken Ruettgers there? Ken was a good football player. Matter of fact, I really thought he should have made the Pro Bowl in '94," He hesitated. "But more so, I used Ken because he was faithful.

"Anyway, do you think *I*, the Lord thy God, need to meet people in *their* place of worship? At their alter of green and gold?"

Wow, those were pretty strong words. I was beginning to feel a little self-righteous and pompous. I didn't think He was talking about me. I've been in church even at kickoff over the last couple of seasons. Then He hit *me* right between the eyes.

"Steve, by the same token, did I need to come to meet you where you were years ago in your church—the tavern?"

As I reflected on His words I didn't feel low, I felt love, real love. It dawned on me like never before just how much rebellion I had been in until He saved me in 1991. I have to admit there is no way I was looking for God. He'd clearly come looking for me. His words knocked the breath out of my chest. I knew what He was saying. He didn't have to rescue me. If I was honest with myself, I had to acknowledge I had been trying to major in Cocktail Hour 101 until six years ago.

I was totally on the same page as He poured more living water out for me to absorb. "When you get back you must share with My special Packer fans and others who will listen that I am trying to share My abounding love with them, the kind that, if reciprocated, can breathe eternal life into them.

"What's happening on that field in Green Bay is not about football. That's just the vehicle, the way I am trying to reach them."

Then He threw out this profound question to take back to the people: "Ask our Packer fan friends this: In a hundred years, will it make a difference to them if the Packers ever won the Super Bowl?"

I was all ears, paralyzed as I listened to the uncompromising truth.

"Steve, tell My beloved people—all that will matter a hundred years from now is where they are. You see, My word says, 'It is appointed unto man once to die and then the judgment.'" He reiterated, "As we know, many Packer fans and others believe if you're good and you die, you go to Green Bay (Heaven), and when you've been bad and die, you go to Dallas. That's fallacy!" He joked.

As serious as a heart attack, He plunged on. "The only way to the Father (Heaven) is through Me, the Son. You can't be good enough to get to Heaven! If they won't believe it, have them read Ephesians 2:8-9. Only I can give eternal life. It is free, but they must choose it. *Tell them*!" Just then, a bolt of lightening flashed and thunder rumbled.

"Please let them know I am waiting for them with My hands outstretched outside the door of their hearts. If anyone hears My voice and lets Me in, I will come in and live in them [Revelations 3:20].

"The second thing to tell people is this: Let them know I have given them a great example, a pure model of a pure, loving relationship. It is the love affair between the Packer players and the fans. Challenge them to take this kind of love and put it into their homes and schools. The churches, too. To leave this example on a football field would be very unfortunate."

I couldn't believe He was saying "the churches." Obviously, He felt we have a long way to go in reflecting His love to the world in the church. This saddened me, but I was convinced it was true as I pondered it.

"Steve, your time is up," He paused. "Now, look at me."

I did, sitting still as a third grader in the principal's office.

"Last, I want you to know and spread this word. *I love Packer fans*! Tell them I love them so much I went to the cross to die for them. To wash away all their sins. If they will surrender their hearts and lives to Me and put their trust and faith in Me as their personal Savior, I will save them. I will forgive them of all their sins. I will also come into their hearts and show them the way to abundant life. That's right, if they call on My name they shall be saved!" [John 6:47].

"One last thing," He said. "Tell people I don't mind all the green and gold, the Packer T-shirts, fingernail polish, and other stuff. But when any of it keeps them out of My church and steps between My relationship with them—well, that's a problem. But I can forgive them, if they accept the words that I have given you."

I quickly rose to my feet and began to walk away. I was really feeling the urgency of His message and was ready to "go back." I had no more questions. Well, just one.

I turned to Him one last time. "I have no doubt as to where I am, here with *You*, Lord, but downstairs . . . was that the . . . Green Bay Packer Hall of Fame?"

"No, my cherished one, you're close. That's the Green Bay Packer . . . Hall of Faith!"

"Oh, yeah. Ooohhh yeaahh."

Then He walked to me and hugged me. As He pressed my head into His chest He whispered, "Sign your books, John 3:3. Now, I will be seeing you soon, time is short, the Kingdom is near. Remember to tell them to go back to My book!"

He drew me closer and then, in a millisecond, in a time span that can't be measured, I awoke. There was a feeling of peace, but also urgency. Was this just a dream? Actually, it wasn't a dream at all—but it is the way God wanted me to tell you of His saving love and grace for all. Friend, are you willing to respond to the Lord's words?

God loves Packer fans. He told me so. In His Word (the Bible) he tells us there's only one ultimate Hall of Fame—Heaven. At Calvary, your debt of sin has been paid in full. And now He has made you the greatest offer ever to meet Him in Heaven. Will you accept Him as your Savior? He's waiting to hear from you. Will you answer Him today? He says your eternal life depends on it. It's your choice. One that's only a leap of faith away.

Chapter 23

The Best of the 1996 "Timeout" Show

I t very well may be the most important sports talk show in the world. Maybe even the most important talk show on the planet! It's called "Timeout." It can be heard each Monday evening from six to seven o'clock during the Packer season on WORQ, 90.1 FM in Green Bay. It began back in 1994.

Beginning that season, I found myself as co-host alongside Ken Ruettgers in Studio A in the "Q's" great broadcast facility. Each week Ken would bring in a teammate to talk about their life, how God had impacted it, and how they were using their platform to help others.

The show can best be described as one that protects the guys from all the uncomfortable questions. The ones they hear all the time. The critical ones. We ask many questions that the mainstream media won't talk about, such as, "What is the Lord doing in your life? How's your family? What's your favorite kind of ice cream? What do you see God doing on the team?"

Over the years people like Sterling Sharpe, (I know—he doesn't do interviews) Bryce Paup, Guy McIntyre, Mark Brunnel, and the current players strolled in for predestined appearances. In my first book it was the section called the Accountability Group. Your feedback said it was the greatest the best part of the book. Thus, we'll rerun some of the tapes for your enjoyment.

Family values, current events, Christian perspectives, testimonies, and other issues have come to the fore in this one-of-a-kind, sixty-minute, weekly gem of a show. Oh sure, occasionally we even talk about football! To our knowledge there is no other radio show like it in any of the NFL cities. Or, for that matter, in all of professional sports.

We know there are many football programs that talk about yardage, interceptions, standings, and other trivia. But have you heard of such a radio program from the rough and tumble world of professional football that sheds light on eternal life? This one does.

From the confines of this studio to the radios of people in Green Bay and the Fox Valley, men who are stereotyped as being too insensitive and rich to mingle with the rest of us choose to bare their souls and plead that they are no different from you and me.

In blue jeans, shorts, T-shirts, sweaters, and tennis shoes, I promise you'd never recognize many of them on the street. I recall meeting Anthony Morgan in the parking lot on Halloween in 1995. If Ken hadn't told me who he was, I never would have known. The same with Lenny McGill who played with the Packers until 1995. They look a bit different in their game-day wardrobe. Helmets have a way of hiding a person's identity.

With Ken Ruettgers facing his serious knee condition, he chose to step aside from the radio program during the 1996 season. John Michels and Don Beebe helped to fill in. We missed the first couple weeks, but we picked up the energy without losing a beat. It was another treasure of memories for the listeners and for me as well. A man by the name of Reggie came in for his first appearance since 1994. The always funny, insightful Pepper Burruss made his third appearance, too.

I have compiled what may be the highlights of the 1996 shows. So come on into the Q-90 studio with us and tune into the radio theater of your mind. Join us for the Best of the 1996 "Timeout" show.

"Timeout" Show #9
with Reggie White and Don Beebe
Monday, December 16, 1996

I was sitting in the spacious downstairs area of the Pro Care Chiropractic Building, which houses the studios of WORQ. I was curled up in one of the soft chairs as I did some preparation for the show. I was curious what player Don Beebe was going to bring in with him. I hadn't talked with him during the week to find out who would be the special guest.

I heard footsteps coming down the stairs. "Hi, Steve," said Don from across the room. He had a friend with him—a big friend—as in Reggie White. It had been two years since Reg had done the show.

"Guys, how you doin?" I asked.

"Great," they answered in harmony.

It had been a while since I'd seen Reggie. I was anxious to get caught up on the news and ask him how his book, *In The Trenches*, and how his movie, "Reggie's Prayer," were doing.

I hopped up and joined them for the short walk down the hall and into the studio. We perched ourselves on chairs. White pulled off his coat to reveal his "Most Valuable Cheesehead" T-shirt. He sat to Beebe's right. I sat to Don's left.

With seven minutes to go to the program intro, I teased Don, "Are you sick of hearing the 'Why didn't you step out of bounds' question, yet?"

"Aw, man," he sighed, blushing just a twinge.

The day before in the Lions game, Don had made a poor decision to stay in bounds after he caught a pass with time running out in the first half. It may have cost the team a field goal. It didn't mean a hill of beans in the final outcome—we won by 31-3—but the media was having a field day with the receiver. I was toying with Don because he had been giving me a rough time on the air the previous weeks. This was my way of having some fun with him. Just bringing it up made me feel better.

Reggie and Don were chatting like a couple sixth-graders when I said, "Sshhh, it's showtime, you guys!" Just then, the guy with the deep voice who did the intro for the show said, "And now, here are your hosts, Don Beebe and Steve Rose, on Q-90 FM."

Pictured, top left: Don Beebe brightens a boy's day with an autograph. (Photo: Courtesy, Neumann Photography) Top right: Steve and 1996 co-host Don Beebe during a break in the "Timeout" show. At bottom: Steve Rose with Reggie White in the WORQ control studio.

Beebe is quietly chanting, "Reggie . . . Reggie . . . Reggie."

We joked around for a while, and then got to the first item on the agenda, Reggie's newly-inked deal to stay in Green Bay for another five years. It was evident just how happy White was to know he would finish his playing career here.

The first thing I wanted Reggie to bring up was how, two years earlier, he and I had sat in this exact spot and talked about how the media was shocked when he told them how God had healed him before the Dallas game on Thanksgiving Day. To refresh your memory, White had hurt his elbow against the Buffalo Bills. He was to miss this game and probably a few more. God had other plans. Reggie and the guys prayed for a miracle and they got it.

A few days later, Reggie and the Packers lost to the Cowboys, but God had been given lots of glory through the testimony of the healing.

The tone of the conversation turned serious as I brought to mind something I recalled from White's December 5, 1994, appearance on the show. It seemed like just yesterday to me.

"Reg, I remember here just a couple years ago we sat and talked about it and you said that had you told the media that you had gone to a witch doctor or had acupuncture—man, they'd have been banging down your door for the phone numbers. But you mention Jesus Christ, there's accountability. People don't want to deal with that, do they, Reggie?" I finished.

"No, they can't deal with that because they can't see it—they can't feel it—they can't touch it. You know and I know it was hard for many people to believe it. But the great thing is a lot of people around this area believed it. It was obvious that God healed me. There were three times that He healed me." said the burly lineman. (The elbow, knee, and hamstring.)

I only recalled the two times we had talked about in the previous book. It was the elbow and hamstring, but Reggie reminded us that God healed his knee after the Minnesota game in the Metrodome. Do you remember when Chris Carter and the guys surrounded him, praying for him? They showed a camera view from the roof and they couldn't believe how both teams were out on the field with him.

Now, had God healed White these times because He wanted the Packers to win? No, we lost to the Cowboys in 1994. Was there a purpose? Yes! Quickly, we talked about the fact that where God is given

His place, He will move. It isn't about wins and losses. We asked Don if he thought this was the case in Green Bay or not.

"Well, I think . . . uh . . . I've always been a firm believer that God doesn't care who wins or loses football games. He's concerned about what's being taught and what lessons are being learned by every individual that knows Christ playing in that game and everybody watching that game. So, there's no doubt God's using the Green Bay Packers this year. I firmly believe that."

To what extent does God really care? Did the fact that God is using the guys guarantee a Super Bowl, just like the other four Beebe has been blessed to play in? He expounded on the thought. "Where it's gonna take us, I don't know, but in the end it's going to be the best result for us. We hope, shoot, I mean we can say we hope it's a Super Bowl Championship, but if it's not a Super Bowl Championship, God's gonna use it in a positive way, I'm sure of that."

Beebe went on to point out that whether a team is loaded with born-again believers really doesn't promise anything. He made a powerful point from his earlier career in Buffalo.

"I'm a person that's lost four Super Bowls and we had a great group of Christians on those teams in Buffalo. Through those years we were able to reach out not only to the people in Buffalo, but all over the country."

He reflected on how Frank Reich, the Bills QB, had been touched by a song Reich heard the morning before engineering the greatest comeback victory in professional football in 1992. (The Bills beat the Oilers 41-38.) Reich had broken down in tears and told the media about it afterward. It was a springboard for further ministry.

White broke in to voice his perspective.

"And I tend to think that at times maybe God does deal in wins and losses. You know people don't listen to losers! When you look at the Bible when men were obedient to God, they were victorious. Our prayer has been, 'Lord, we don't want to win so we can get a pat on the back so that people can tell us how great we are. We wanna win to honor You! We try to keep that in mind when we go out on the field. It may be for that one life up in the stands. That's the way we try to look at it."

White acknowledged that without taking the thrill of winning games the year before for granted, they wanted to kick it up a notch from the ministry side of things. That they expected to win and were looking more at the big picture.

"The more we win, the more exposure we get, the more opportunities we have to honor God. That's the situation we're working for. That's why we have so many guys on this team who are working so hard towards that goal."

"It's not about the ring, it's about God's glory," I added.

"Exactly," chimed the big man.

I wanted to address the issue of just how far we as fans are supposed to go to show our allegiance, loyalties, and love for this team without stepping on God's plans for our lives. I had been traveling the country telling people and reminding myself that we need to keep the Packermania stuff in perspective. I looked forward to hearing some feedback from the guys. Don went first.

"First of all, I think the emotion of going to the Super Bowl and all that is great. I mean, you ask any Packer, we love it. Everything in your life needs to be put into perspective. Obviously, Christ comes first, then your family, and then friends and stuff like that."

I became a tad impatient and was really looking for one of the fellas to help me build the case that sometimes we get lost a little too far in this team. Don continued and showed a little frustration in my belaboring the point.

"It's OK for you, but what about those fans who may be setting themselves up by taking it to an extreme?" I inquired.

"Well, I mean, what's an extreme? I mean if somebody is going to get hurt out of it, sure, but I've seen people coming over to the stadium every day, no I . . . ."

I interrupted with, "I'm talking about the people who may be missing church services on Sunday to come and see the game."

Reggie came and filled a gaping hole in the discussion.

"The Bible says God will use the foolish things of the world. I mean, it's fun, but it's foolish in a way what we do, but God will use whatever He wants to use to honor His name. Last year, I had some friends come to a game and they were touched by the people singing along to the song, 'Amazing Grace' on the Jumbotron, you had people that were . . . drunk, that were crying."

Reggie has never kept it a secret why he loves the Packer fans and people of Wisconsin so much. He expounded on the issue for a moment.

"The thing I like about the people here that cheer for us is that they take what we say seriously, they don't take it for granted. If we say, 'Jesus is Lord,' they believe it. Those have been the supernatural things up here. As we started being successful, people started identifying this team with what God was doing and not what we're accomplishing," said a beaming White.

I thought we needed to lighten things up just a little bit when Scotty, our faithful engineer, signaled there was a telephone call. It was Rob, from Appleton, on the line for Don.

He began, "Don, I just wanted you to know that I was at Christ the Rock the other night when you and Keith Jackson spoke. I really appreciated your words that night."

Beebe showed his gratitude humbly by acknowledging, "Rob, I really appreciate that. It was a lot of fun."

Rob had some great news for Beebe.

"I just wanted to inform you that evening, as a result of your and Keith Jackson's message, we had sixty people choose to accept Christ as their Lord and Savior. Additionally, there are forty others who requested more information."

"Aw . . . that's great news. As I said that night, that's what it's all about. That's why guys like Reggie, Keith Jackson, and I are in this . . . let's call it . . . business. God put us here for a reason. We have a platform and that's to reach people for Jesus Christ," said the fleet-of-foot Packer.

I wish you could have been there to hear Don Beebe's next words. They have been captured on tape. They are words that should be played for anyone who claims that many of these guys are out for themselves and the dollar. Don brought things to perspective with these words:

"It's not about the fame and money and all that stuff. My main objective is to reach people for Jesus Christ."

Now words only mean so much, but by now anybody who has followed Don Beebe since the Super Bowl win will tell you just how bent he is on getting out and sharing his heart with others.

Julie from Chilton called. She was at Christ the Rock too.

"Don, you can count us in on a couple of those people who chose to follow Christ the night you spoke. I don't want to embarrass my husband, who is listening out in the barn, but your message was very strong."

Reggie White talked about the pressure he feels as a professional athlete to minister to everyone else's needs. "Most people think 'cause we're athletes and Christians that we're supposed to be out on the speaking circuit and telling everybody about Jesus. We do, but we have families also that we have to minister to. If we minister to everybody else except our family, then we're missing the whole point."

He did tell of one huge fear that he has, however.

"My fear, I'll admit, is that I'll go through this life and take certain things for granted, and somebody will die and go to hell because I didn't do exactly what God wanted me to do. That's a scary thought." Powerful words from a powerful man who feels that at times he isn't doing enough. His actions show otherwise.

Christina from Appleton then called with some great comments and questions for the guys.

"How is it to be distracted by fame? How easy is it to take the glory for yourself?"

Reggie paused and then commented, "Well, it's . . . [he looked at Beebe with a big grin] . . . We got two wives that keep us in check!" Everybody roared.

"When we were younger, and I think I speak for Donny, too, I mean the fame and the fortune can get to you."

I thought his next words were especially wise.

"I tell guys all the time that I'm ministering to on the team, 'Don't think that women like you because you look good. [Giggles from all of us.] 'They like you 'cause your pocket's fat! The devil can deceive us and make us think we're more than who we are. That's why I thank people like Don and others who help to keep us in line."

Christina brought up a great point, that she had developed a new-found respect for the guys on the team because of the way they pray on the field. Not only with their teammates, but with the opponent. This had given her a new respect for what the guys were doing. I especially appreciated another point she made: "I was just telling my husband, the last time we were watching you play on Sunday, that I believe you are succeeding and winning because God is putting you in the limelight."

The issue of idolatry and priorities came back one more time as she made another strong point. "It may be more socially acceptable to paint your face and belly green and run around wearing a Cheesehead hat and run down the street screaming 'Packers are number one!' than it is to walk up to someone with a cross around your neck and say, 'Jesus saves.'" Amen.

Reggie added that he felt fans are attracted to football because it is perceived as fun, whereas so many of the things associated with following Christ are not fun. Reggie added this: "Back in the day of Pentecost, people had found they enjoyed worshipping God. We need to set it in a way where young people in particular enjoy coming to church. The kids don't always see that we're God's disciples 'cause they don't see our love for one another."

Christina finished her thoughts by saying, "Well, the kids are seeing you guys in prayer, being cool and being holy at the same time, so it's no longer an oxymoron."

As the commercial break music played under my voice, I announced the phone numbers and the sponsors, and then said,"Reggie White . . . unarguably the greatest Christian in all of professional sports, whom God has given a great platform which he stands on proudly, and Don Beebe—four Super Bowls, yet to get a ring, and hopefully this year will be the year he gets one . . . he's here also . . . we're back right after this on Q-90 on the 'Timeout' program."

During the break, you would have thought we were a bunch of sixth graders. Reggie and Don began picking on each other.

"Reggie, you sure talk a lot!" said Beebe.

"That's 'cause you won't say anything," White laughed.

As we came back from the break I mentioned Don Beebe's name and Reggie playfully chanted, "Bee-bee-bee-bee-bee!"

Those of us in Wisconsin have watched Reggie pitching Ford truck commercials on TV. In the commercials, White is shown as being play fully submissive to his wife Sara. I had always wondered just how accurate that representation was.

"Reggie, you made a comment here before, saying you have a wonderful wife at home who keeps you accountable, so there's a lot of truth to those commercials that say, 'Hey, Sugar, can I get another truck?'"

"Yeah, I gotta beg her for a truck. In public, I tell people I'm the man, but when I get home, it's different," he joked.

I believe that he really wasn't joking.

"Ain't that right, Donny," he beamed at Beebe.

"That's right, Buddy," chuckled Don with no hesitation what-soever. "That just goes back to priorities, which we were talking about earlier."

Al from Green Bay then asked Reggie how God had helped him in his football career and in his life. The lineman said that it couldn't be measured. Mainly, he'd learned that in order to succeed you must be willing to pay the price and work hard. Mental toughness, he thought, was one of the great gifts from the Lord. Also, Reggie was very grate-ful to God for the chance to honor Him through his football career.

White continued to very forthcoming as Al asked, "Do you have to work harder after you're a Christian or before?"

"I tell people it's much more difficult after you become a Christ-ian because it was so much easier to do what was wrong. When you become a Christian, that's when all the temptations come in and you have to make up your mind if you're going to fall into it or not." He wasn't through.

"You know, I used to tell people that when you become saved [accept Jesus Christ as Lord and Savior] that it's easy, God finally spoke to me and said, 'You're lying!' It is not easier. I think it takes a real man and a real woman who is willing to do whatever it takes to serve God and shake up the mainstream and serve our God."

Finally, it came out, and it was Al who asked, "And I just wanted to ask why Don didn't go out of bounds!"

"He's heard that enough," I jumped in.

"No, I'm just teasing ya!"

"Get him off the radio right now," joked White.

"We're going over to Elkhart Lake for our next call," I quipped.

Looking over his left shoulder at me, Don inquired, "You mean I don't get to respond to that guy?"

White thought that was great. I'm sure he could appreciate it, too.

Finally, we let Gretchen from Elkhart Lake come into the program via the telephone.

"I just wanted to thank you guys for kneeling down and praying after you guys make touchdowns and stuff. It's awesome to see you guys out there and praying, it's a good testimony."

"Thanks for the comments," said Beebe. "When I kneel down it's not to glorify myself in any way. It's to glorify God. If you've ever heard my story of where I've come from and what God has brought me through, there's no way I should be playing in my eighth year in the NFL. Without his grace I wouldn't be here, there's no doubt. So I just take the opportunity every time I score to thank God for the opportunities He's giving me."

The caller asked whether Don and Reggie had the opportunity to say anything to President Clinton when he appeared at Lambeau Field earlier in the season.

"We didn't get an opportunity to talk about the Lord or policies with him. There were about a hundred security guys around him."

Being a conservative Christian, we asked whether White felt uncomfortable around a man who expressed some views different from his. This is what he said: "I learned a long time ago not to be scared of people because of what they believe. I believe that if we prayed more at home we wouldn't have the problems in our schools—if we all got onto Jesus' agenda and went right to the people and ministered to them. Because of that, many people discovered who He was, and their lives changed. We want to change the social structure of our country, and fighting over certain issues is not going to do that. Helping people's lives will."

I had some thoughts on the issue. "So many times we try to change people, but I think if we will pray for God to change us, then we can make a difference. Like with me, when Christ came in, that's when the alcohol, nicotine, gambling, and other stuff left. Jesus heals," I finished. Reggie agreed. "You're exactly right. We try to do what God said He will do. When we see a person get into some sin, we get on that person, and God is saying, 'Wait a minute . . . I'm God, he's Mine!' "

Just when it seemed as if the range of questions couldn't get any better, Joe came in and asked Reggie this: "I heard you say recently you became a preacher too early, and I wonder if you would comment on that?"

"Yeah, I did. At the time I remember I was sixteen or seventeen years old. I remember telling my mother I was going to be a preacher and a football player. My mother could understand the football player, but she couldn't understand the preaching part."

Reggie did start preaching at seventeen. It was then that a spirit descended on him, one that wanted to destroy him.

"When I decided I wanted to preach, that's when I started doing all kinds of bad things. It's like the devil said, 'OK, all those things he wants to do, and all those things he wants to be, I'm gonna send them to him.'"

He went to the book of First Timothy to read about the qualifications of a minister, and it was here where he realized that he had jumped the gun a bit.

"It said that a preacher should not be a new convert. I look back and I didn't have anybody teaching me. I didn't have anybody discipling me. And that's when I fell into the trap of the enemy and I became very prideful. I felt that if Billy Graham and I were in the same room, and I was witnessing to someone, that Billy Graham needed to be quiet and let Reggie talk."

Here was the big teddy bear laying it out that he was prideful, and without Christ would become prideful again. He had some great advice to anyone who feels the calling to preach. "You must be discipled. You must get a teacher. You must have a mentor, and you must allow God to lead you instead of allowing people to lead you."

The next caller asked how hard it is for a football player to celebrate Christmas, a holiday when many are away playing in big games.

Beebe responded, "I've always felt that as a football player [he looked at White] we don't know what holidays are." White concurred with his husky laugh. He thanked his family for their support during the holiday seasons.

We couldn't let Reggie get away without professing some hope regarding the churches in the South that had burned the year before, including his home church in Tennessee where he is an associate pastor, and other churches around the country that had been torched.

I said, "Reggie, I remember you saying a year ago that Satan could not get away with this stuff without something good happening. For instance, look at the people who reached out." White got fired up with the hope which he has always felt from the people of Wisconsin.

"The people up here have shown me the type of love and respect that as you grow older you are searching for. That was one of the reasons I wanted to sign here. People from all around the country, but mostly from up here, said to Reggie White through their actions that they weren't doing this for Reggie White the football player. We're doing this because of the type of person you are."

He was somewhat disappointed in the way that many Christians reacted during this time of need. He thought the country was too slow to jump in and help. He said we should have come to the rescue of the brethren when they needed us most, right at the beginning.

The subject of revival was brought to White's attention, and much like many other times, he gave his explanation of why he was brought to Green Bay and just what the Almighty may be up to. It was an incredibly bold statement:

"I am feeling revival in many places around the country, but mostly up here [inWisconsin]. I believe God sent me and people like Don Beebe and Keith Jackson here to, number one, change the perception of the team. Two, that God trusted the people of Wisconsin. When Jesus sent the disciples out He said do these two things. Eat whatever is put before you, and heal the sick, and tell them the kingdom of God is near."

The people of Wisconsin can take these next words and put them on their mantles. If you had a suspicion that Reggie believes in you and loves you, then this will confirm it.

"The people of this state, from the richest to the poorest, have accepted the word of God. I've been invited by organizations that are not Christian organizations, and when I go there it's packed, and I preach. They don't give me any restrictions and say we don't want you talking about that stuff. They call me Reverend White. I'd rather have them call me Reggie, but everywhere I go they show me respect enough to call me Reverend White. Up here, I've been able to preach without restrictions." Right here is where White sums up why the word of God is being spread through football in Wisconsin, which has springboarded it to the world.

"I tell people that the reason God would send Reggie White to Green Bay, Wisconsin is because He knew the people of the state would react in a way that they wouldn't have in San Francisco or Dallas. They would receive the word of God in a way that would cause a revival in this state. And also so they could serve as an example for the rest of this country."

"Football is just the platform," I added.

"Exactly!"

I started to plug Reggie's book, *In The Trenches*, when White butted in and said, "Is Donny always this quiet, or am I talking too much?"

"Hey, I'm just enjoying listening to you, bro!"

Reggie issued another belly laugh.

We chatted about the pressure of having everyone wanting you. "Reggie, what's that like?" I inquired.

"You know, I can handle the pressure. The tough part is when you want to be with your family, when you want to be a husband, when you want to go out to eat with your wife. That's hard because people invade your privacy."

In my four years around these guys I have never heard a bolder statement about the problems of being a superstar than the one White gave us that night. "If people invade my privacy, I may end up being rude," he said. "I don't want to be rude. My kids are important to me. I'm not trying to brush people off in any kind of way. People need to understand, I'm a father and a husband.

"It's hard for me when I go home and my wife tells me the kids have been wondering why daddy hasn't been doing this and that with us . . . it's hard. That's why sometimes I have to be rude, to keep my family's attention, and I have to let them know that I love them, no matter what, and I have to show them that in public."

Next time any of us sees one of the guys at the Prime Quarter or Backgammon's Pub, let's keep this in mind.

Mike in Little Chute was waiting patiently on the phone, and he came up with another great question.

"I'm aware there are a large number of Christians on the team. I am aware that you have large Bible studys. But, what's the accountability? Can anybody on the team go up to Reggie and say, 'Reggie, as a Christian, this just doesn't seem right?'"

Don began. "I think that conversation is going on all the time. I think not only are we reaching out to the community, but to our teammates. I'm not going to mention any names, but there have been many guys on the team who have either accepted Christ, or rededicated their lives. I think that's really neat. We do have a lot of Bible studys and we are accountable to each other. Many different people on this team have the right and I want them to tell me if they see something in my life that isn't right."

He went on to tell us that if he felt the need to confront Reggie White, he would, and vice-versa. He noted that it's not about judging, but about accountability. Beebe said he has an understanding with everyone in his family that they will ask the tough questions.

White agreed with Beebe. "If I do something wrong, I want the brothers in the Lord to come up to me and let me know. I may not agree with them at the time. There have been many times I have been corrected that I didn't agree with it at the time, but when I woke up the next morning I've realized that they were right. My wife and pastor do a great job of keeping me accountable."

White recalled one incident where he and Sara sat down with their pastor.

"I thought, 'Boy, he's going to be all over her!' " he recalled. But Reggie was very much mistaken. "For two hours he was all over me! He asked me later if I was mad at him and I said, 'Yeah—but you know what? You were right! Everything you said was right. And I know you told me because you love me, so I know you're right and I'll get over it tomorrow.'"

Even Reggie White is wrong every now and then. Imagine that!

It was nearly time for another break, when I asked, "Hey, did we play a football game yesterday?" Beebe was teasing Reggie, and Reggie was starting to lose it.

"Reggie is losing it, and we're going to put him back on his chair," I said, as the theme music started, indicating that it was time for a commercial break. Beebe slapped White on the shoulder and then in a real husky voice ala White, he whispers, "Heyyy!" You could hear Reggie snort real loud into the microphone! What a couple of goofballs. I wish you could have been there.

We joked about how Robert Brooks was having a good time doing soap operas and "Wheel of Fortune" while the other guys were "working."

"He certainly would like to be with us," noted Beebe.

One thing I had never known, which Reggie talked about in his book, was how he wound up in Green Bay. It was the story of how he felt that God wanted him in San Francisco, but he felt he was supposed to be in Green Bay. God miraculously showed him that he really belonged in Green Bay. It's a wild story.

One more time we want to let the guys talk about who has touched Reggie and the guys. They are the greatest fans in the world—Packer fans!

"When you came up here in July of 1993, and sixty thousand people came to watch a scrimmage, what did you think?" I asked.

"It blew my mind," Don admitted. "Not only did that blow my mind, but I knew that over the twenty-year period the team was losing they were still playing in front of sellout crowds. I got convinced then that these were the best fans in the world!"

When asked, both White and Beebe agreed that Dallas was the best team in the NFC. But the beginning of the end with these overgrown young men arrived when I made the mistake of asking them both, "Who is the best team in the AFC?"

Without missing a beat Don said, "Buffalo." Reggie let out a facetious yell as Beebe favored his former teammates.

"Who do you think is, Reggie?"

A bit apologetic to Beebe he said, "I think it's Denver."

As Beebe started to talk, Reggie playfully interrupted, saying, "Did you tell them what Jim Kelly and those guys sent you after the Detroit game?" The fragile Beebe had his bell rung twice during that game. The hits would have killed most gorillas.

"Go ahead, Reggie, tell them."

As White stumbled and stammered to come up with the words for what he was trying to say to describe the gift sent to Beebe, Don began mocking the big fella. "Uhhh . . . whaaa whaa wha."

"It was one of those extra helmets!" said Reggie. It was a protective bubble-type of helmet that players like Steve Wallace have worn for extra protection. Don had concussions in Buffalo in the early nineties and wore a red one there.

Beebe countered, "That's it, I'm digging up dirt on you. I'm digging up dirt!"

"I'm just tellin' what they did," said Reggie. "They love you. They wanted to protect you."

Beebe wasn't convinced of White's sincerity. "I know you better than that!"

I made the mistake of throwing myself into the mix at Beebe's expense. "They can call him, 'Bubble Beebe.'"

"The thing about it was that it was red. It would have looked really funny with a red helmet on top of a yellow one."

I changed the subject to the Carolina Panthers, to bail out my co-host.

White said he felt that Carolina was going to be tough, that they couldn't accept the fact that they were an expansion team. Then he began to crack up, because Beebe was making a face at him. The trouble had begun!

"Did you ever notice that Reggie talks a lot?" said Don.

"Hey, you won't talk!" responded Reggie.

Beebe moaned and groaned, as if he had been trying to get in a word edgewise.

"When Reg talks, people listen," I proclaimed. "Reggie, talk about the Dallas stuff that happened earlier when they kicked the field goal."

"Go ahead, Donny, I'm leaving," he joked.

Time was just about up. I think we were lucky to quit while we were still all in one piece. There were a couple of choice barbs yet to be thrown. We debated about taking one more telephone call, and then Scotty, our producer, shook his head, indicating there was no more time.

"We gotta go. Maybe we can get Reggie to come back sometime after the Super Bowl."

"I don't think Donny will let me, no more!" cried Reggie.

"Anybody got a tissue? Where's the tissue?" Beebe asked. With friends like Beebe, Reggie didn't need enemies.

Then Don seriously told his friend, "You were the greatest guest I've had all year. I mean that, you are . . . you're great!"

With the theme music in the background, pushing us out the door, Reggie had one more sympathetic remark. "Donny just told me I ain't coming back no more."

"I'm only coming with my red bubble head!" laughed Beebe.

All were friends in the end. "Pray for Reggie and Don that God's will would be done in their lives, and let's hope that's a Super Bowl victory. So, thanks for coming in. For Reggie White and Don Beebe, I am the highly uneducated Steve Rose. We're back at you again next week."

As the music trailed, Reggie could be heard mumbling, "Let's do this again."

Man, I hope so. We all had a ball.

After the show, Reggie posed in his deep green "Most Valuable Cheesehead" T-shirt for a picture with me. It's a great shot of us. The thing I remember most from that night, however, was Reggie's humor, how he couldn't help losing it, both during the show and the breaks. He just thought everything was funny. His giggle is something you have to hear at least once.

You know, so often you only get to see the serious side of the guys, and especially Reggie White. Let me tell you, he can be a gas. If only you knew how badly these guys would like to let it rip, let their hair down, and get rid of the serious images we have of them.

This night he and Beebe did just that.

"Timeout" Show #2
Steve Rose with Ken Ruettgers
Monday, October 21, 1996
as told by Bob Gardinier

I was pumped. Scotty, from WORQ, had called me at my Oshkosh office to inform me I'd be working with my friend Ken Ruettgers this night for the "Timeout" show. Ken had been nursing his injured knee and was putting all his energies into rehabilitation. This meant he'd also be taking a break from co-hosting the "Timeout" show with me. So, we had done a couple weeks without him, with Don Beebe and John Michels filling in.

It had been a while since I'd talked to Ken and even longer since I'd seen him. Probably six months. That's why I was thrilled to hear of the news. I wasn't disappointed. It was just like old times. I wish the show could have lasted all night!

Keep in mind, this show was a month before Ken had to tearfully call it quits as a player. He was rehabbing diligently. Truthfully, I thought by the twinkle Kenny had in his eye that night——well, I would have sworn he knew he was going to be able to pull it off and play. We all know what happened, and we may never understand why he wasn't able to join his friends in the Super Dome in New Orleans.

For this segment, I have asked my friend and faithful servant, Bob Gardinier to sit in and talk about this night. I feel he can capture for you what I objectively can't. I think I'm a little too close to it, and maybe a tad giddy, too.

Sit back and enjoy as Bob brings the warmth of this October reunion back to life—for both of us:

It was mid-morning on a Thursday in late June, as I sat at my computer. Just days earlier, Steve Rose had crowned me the Director of

Network Development for the Winners Success Radio Network, a divison of his personal development company called the Winners Success Network. My job is to take the "Timeout" radio program and launch it to a statewide, and eventually, to a nationwide audience.

On this particular morning, Steve seemed more excited than usual. Sometimes his excitable nature is good, other times it's a sign to proceed with caution. I had a lot of work in my "in" basket and I was afraid Steve had his "idea machine" working overtime, which can mean more work for those around him . . . which means me!

What is Steve's idea machine? Quite simply it's Steve's mind. Rest assured that if the circus were as popular today as it was in P.T. Barnum's day, Steve would have the greatest show on earth. You see, just like ol' P.T., Steve is an idea person, and when he gets excited— look out!

Seconds later, Steve was asking me if I'd be interested in transcribing one of the "Timeout" programs from tape to print and giving him my thoughts.

My mind was racing as I wondered if I had heard him correctly. Was Steve asking me to contribute something to his latest book project that might end up in print?

"Sure," I said, even though I didn't know where I'd find the time. I'd just finished writing the manuscript for my own book and was in search of a publisher. Between that, family, and church activities as well as the launch of the new network, what was I to say? Then all of a sudden, Steve got that gleam in his eyes.

Steve knew that I'd been closely connected with the *Leap of Faith* projects and that I was quite familiar with the "Timeout" program. It came as no surprise, at that point, when Steve proceeded to ask me to write a chapter for this book based on one of the "Timeout" tapes. Specifically, it was the one of Steve and Ken. He wanted a good neutral observation of his special relationship with Ken. Admittedly, the guy could be Ruettgers' publicist. Steve thinks a lot of him.

He had a point. I was close to the projects, but not so close so as to be intertwined personally with the show and Ken. My point of view could show *you*, the reader, that Steve really is being honest about the quality and character of Ken Ruettgers and the other green and gold gargantuans we call the Green Bay Packers.

Ken Ruettgers and Steve Rose having some fun in the hall of the WORQ studios in Green Bay.

"You're on!" I said. After all, Steve and I have been through a lot in the past. Steve lives what he preaches and I wanted him to continue to succeed. The word "servanthood," a word I had become very familiar with through the writings of K.P. Yohannan from *Gospel for Asia*, kept ringing in my head.

What an honor and a privilege. After all, how many writers would put aside a portion of their platform to make room for the thoughts and feelings of someone else? That's just the kind of person Steve Rose is—unselfish and giving, a man who believes not only in his own success but the success of those around him as well. This is why I'm proud to call Steve Rose a great friend.

So here it is for you to enjoy, one of the most memorable moments from the 1996 "Timeout" series.

Absence makes the heart grow fonder. This was never more apparent as Steve opened up this edition of the "Timeout" program. You see, Ken and Steve, the original duo to host the program, had not seen each other for approximately nine months.

As the program opened, Steve explained to Ken that the guys at the radio station called to say that Ken would be back in the saddle to co-host that evening. It was obvious that Steve was delighted to have Ken back, and Ken was pleased, too.

It's that spirit of friendship, unity, and comraderie that launched this edition of the program into its first order of business—Ken's fallen comrade, Robert Brooks. Brooks had suffered a season-ending knee injury the previous week against the San Francisco 49ers. You could hear the great care and concern in the hosts' voices as Steve began the discussion.

"I think a lot of the Romans 8:28 thing is so appropo when you talk about the fact that Robert's out. Why Robert Brooks? A guy who works hard, a guy who deserves to be Super Bowl bound just as you do, Ken, and all of a sudden he's hurt," said Steve. He went on to make a point about Brooks he'd made in his book, *Leap of Faith: God Must Be A Packer Fan*. "The guy epitomized the Packers last year in this love-bonding thing. Peter King, from *Sports Illustrated*, told me that in his twelve years covering the NFL, Ken, he never saw player-fan bonding like he saw last year."

Ken responded, "Well, sure, and I think Green Bay is a perfect place for that. You've got the community, and it's a close-knit bunch and it's a good Midwest city and coming from California and being in Los Angeles, most of the fans out there really couldn't care less about the players.

"When the Raiders were out there, they [the fans] were more into seeing movie stars, and so it's really neat to see the fans so involved with the players, and on the same level. That gap does not exist in Green Bay like it does in other NFL cities."

If you're still not convinced about this player-fan bonding environment, let Ken Ruettgers explain it to you.

"First of all, I have to thank the fans out there because I've gotten inundated with so much great fan mail, faxes, and messages left on the voice mail. It's from people that I know, and many I don't know, wishing me the best. They are writing and saying they've been praying for me."

Ken continued, "And a lot of real neat letters saying they've been praying for God's will, which is what I've been praying for obviously, because that's my perspective as where we should be. And it's so tempting to say, 'God healed me,' but you know if He truly knows what's best for me and He has His hand in this decision, which I believe He has His hands in our lives and destinies, then it really is easy for me to go out and work as hard as I can to get back knowing He's in full control.

"I really tried to avoid having surgery in the off-season, but it's one of those things where I had to have a couple of pieces taken out that were floating around and right away even though I didn't participate in the mini-camps."

Then Ruettgers made this comment. And one could tell by the sound of his voice he wasn't saying it in a cliche tone. He remarked, "I could see from the sidelines while I was present at the mini-camps, this team is going to the Super Bowl."

Reggie White may be the team healer, but what did that make Ken Ruettgers? The team prophet? Typically, throughout his career, the Wisconsin media had portrayed Ken as a hard-working, conservative figure, not the Packers' version of Moses, ready to lead the Pack into the promised land.

As we all know, Ken was right. The Pack won the Super Bowl, but as a Ken Ruettgers fan, my feelings were mixed because he wasn't playing.

Have you ever had to wait for something? I mean really wait for what seemed like an eternity? Imagine what Ken had to deal with, confident the Packers would win the Super Bowl, yet having to be patient because of knee problems. What kept him on the right track?

"Eugene Robinson, Don Beebe, all the guys have been so encouraging and uplifting and it is a difficult situation. Some teams would not be that way so I'm very thankful for that encouragement," said Ken. "I think they know I'm doing everything that I can in trying to figure out how to undo the combination so I can get back on that field and get through that door and get back out there."

The callers that evening made the program truly an international affair as evidenced by Buddy from Vancouver, B.C., Canada. The conversation went like this:

"I can't believe I'm on this show!" exclaimed Buddy.

"Well we can't believe we have you here all the way from Vancouver!" replied Steve.

"Well, I have been a Packer fan since I was nine years old. The last time I saw a Green Bay Packer game was in 1973, I think at Lambeau Field when they retired Ray Nitschke's sweater. That's how far back I go. I just want to say one thing. First of all, Steve, I read your book, *Leap of Faith*, and it was one of the most inspiring, well-written books I've ever read in my life and I want to congratulate you for it.

"I've given it out to some of my pals in Vancouver and it was just fabulous, just fabulous, and when I finished reading it, I said, 'Well, I have to get the telephone number of WORQ just to try and get on the line.' Again, thank you for putting out a book this wonderful, but even more so, just sharing my enthusiasm about Green Bay's year.

"Just to show you how crazy I am, I mean there are Canadian Packer fans out there, believe me, I've already made my reservations at the [Green Bay] Raddison Hotel for January 10th, 11th, and 12th." [Steve and Ken laughed slyly.]

"I said to my son when he was born, just to show you how far back I go, I ordered Packer clothes for this kid when he was born nine years ago, from Bertrand's Sport Shop in Green Bay."

"Oh yeah, sure, Bertrand's," said Ken.

"And I said to him every year, I said if they ever get into the NFC Championship at Lambeau Field, I said it's been twenty-three years but we are there. We are there!

Top picture: "Steve, stand up!" Darius Holland (#90) and Ken Ruettgers (right) dwarf Steve Rose. Steve says this is his favorite picture of all time. Bottom picture: Keith Jackson and Ken Ruettgers with Steve at the WORQ studios.

"I know it's tough to get tickets but God willing, I'll get them, but even if I don't, the hotel reservations are made, the airline tickets are bought."

"Well, come out and tailgate with us," yelled Ken.

"I booked my reservations . . ."

"That's half the fun anyway!" interrupts Ken.

Steve, looking for his turn, asks, "Can he come here for a taping of the show, Ken?"

"Yeah man, who knows? The Super Bowl edition or NFC Championship edition in the parking lot!"

"Ken and I are going to invite you right now to a taping of the 'Timeout' program with us," said Steve. "You can be a special guest here."

"I'm going to tell you, I'm a securities analyst here in Vancouver, and right around my wall there is nothing but Packer memorabilia. I think it was about twenty years ago I asked Lee Remmel to send me some shots of Vince Lombardi, who's been my all-time idol.

"That's how I started following the team at nine years old. My father told me there's some guy that's coming from the Giants over to the Packers and watch what this guy will do with them. I was an ardent Giants fan because I grew up in Montreal and all of a sudden I started following the Packers and it became religious. That's why I related so much to your book. I'm not trying to give you too many plugs on the air for your book . . ."

"Oh, that's OK, there's no limit," laughed Steve.

"Believe me, there were no bags over my head during the lean years. I guarantee you, it was always next year and next year and next year."

"We know—it's worse than the Cubs," replied Steve.

"Last year we all had a taste of it, but Brooks or no Brooks, I honestly believe, God willing, this guy will be back for the playoffs. In spite of that, everyone steps up and there is no question in my mind, when I made those reservations for Lambeau and for the Radisson Hotel, it was crazy. I said to myself, 'I am there! I am there! This is their year. *Come to papa!*'

"There are Canadian Packer fans that love them just as much as you guys do," continued Buddy, "and everything that you say in this book is true. We love them because they're more than just a football team. They have a connection with their fans that is something that you just can't describe and I'm a living testament to it."

As a Packer fan I thank the Lord that Ken did continue playing. It wasn't for as long a period as I would have liked for ol' number 75, but there may have been an eternal reason for this.

Let's face it. When offensive linemen the quality of Ken Ruettgers are doing their job, not much is said about them. Ken's mid-season retirement may have been God's way of drawing people's attention to something much larger than even Ken's career on the field. I believe God wanted people to see Ken's perseverance, patience, faith, and ministry.

Did Ken receive a Super Bowl ring? Yes he did! When the final gun sounds on our lives, I feel that Ken would want us to follow his example and finish the race the apostle Paul talked about in Acts 20:24.

As Buddy from Vancouver shows us, it doesn't matter from what part of the world you support the Packers. Follow Ken's example of perseverance, patience, and faith in Jesus and you, too, will receive your prize, the crown of glory that awaits those who trust in Christ as Savior and Lord.

How does a person go about doing this? If you were to meet Ken Ruettgers for the first time, it could happen in the following manner, as we peek into the second half of this classic "Timeout" episode:

Ken says, "It's been fun, because about four weeks ago I was reading a book and it asked, "If you were to die today . . . [Steve joins in, in unison with Ken] . . . and stand before God, and He should ask you, 'Why should I let you into My Heaven?' what would you say?"

"It's poignant, isn't it?" asks Steve.

"It really makes you have to get real and get down deep," says Ken. "All the people I hang around with now are Christians and they know all the right answers.

"When I came out of the locker room the last four or five weeks, it's amazing, the number of people that are waiting after a regular work day to get an autograph for an answer to that question.

"It's surprising because when you're in the Christian culture, and everybody knows the right answers to the right questions, you forget how many lost souls there are out there, or just the perspective people have, because, 'I'm a Packer fan.'"

Steve chimed in. "Ken Ruettgers, holding his autograph hostage for these eternal questions, I tell ya! [both laughing] This is supposed to be about football!"

"It's a fun time," replied Ken, "rather than just signing autographs, to get a chance to talk to people about something as important . . ."

Steve interrupted, "I've seen this guy in a coffee shop walk up to a group of people and say, 'What do you guys think of this God thing?' I mean, this guy, bold as gold—the devil does hate it."

"Yeah, people say I'm going to Heaven because I'm good . . ."

"Do you hear the Ten Commandments answer?" asked Steve.

"Yeah, or because I go to church or some church tradition that I've done. It's really neat because it opens the door for a great discussion."

Please don't wait to meet Ken Ruettgers to get the answer to the eternal life question. Study the greatest playbook ever, the Bible, and you, too, will discover the secret to the success of many of today's great Packer heroes.

"Timeout" Show #7
Adam Timmerman
with John Michels and Steve Rose
December 2, 1996

There was more beef in the studio than the local meat locker when Adam Timmerman joined John Michels and me on "Timeout." Actually, it was half of the Packer offensive line! It was a roller coaster as two of the most humble men in Green Bay green honored us with their presence on the airwaves.

The newness of everything was still apparent when talking to the second-year lineman Timmerman and the rookie Michels. You could feel how fortunate they felt just to be a part of the team.

Enjoy the fun and the mayhem, but also listen to the message that reminds us that this is just a game—that the most important things are those which cannot be seen. I think the message came out loud and clear that night.

Pay close attention to how Michels described his reaction to the pressures that worshipping fans can put on the team, including himself.

Well, without further ado . . .

We first teased John Michels about being a rookie and then I asked him if he knew where Timmerman's hometown of Cherokee, Iowa, was. He didn't.

"John, I've been there, it's not the end of the world—but you can see it from there!" I joked.

"You can smell it from there!" John teased his fellow lineman.

"No, you can't quite smell California from there," Adam retorted quickly. "We can see the state of Iowa end to end—it's not smog-filled. What can I say?"

"That's true," admitted Michels.

The next order of business was the prominence of Timmerman's acting career, at least the existence of it. I told the audience how I knew Timmerman before he began doing those Chevy commercials. In the spots the burly one looks at the camera after his wife Jana has spoken a few lines and all he says is, "Chevy."

"Adam, how long did it take you to learn those lines, anyway?"

"That's my tough line. At least two weeks. Yeah, it's really astounding how long it took. There were lots of negotiations—and of course, acting school," he said.

"My wife did a better job than I did. It took her about two takes, mine about twenty-two," he chuckled. "I can attest to the fact that there has never been greater meaning to the phrase 'beauty and the beast,' trust me."

One of the cuter subplots to one of the thirty-second TV commercials is that Jana is carrying Adam's huge bag of equipment.

We teased John about his upcoming wedding. Adam admitted he wasn't an expert yet, having been married only a couple of years. And me, well, my wife nearly died laughing when I once told her I was considering doing some marriage counseling as a sideline.

We launched into discussion of one of the great annual practical jokes that expose a few Packer turkeys, ah, rookies. Each year, the team has a little fun, at the expense of a few blushing players.

Each season, an official Packer memo is put in the lockers of each of the rookies. It says the team will be providing turkeys at a local gocery store, but they must go get them. The memo says they will be providing turkeys, not buying them.

Well, the rookie shows up with a cart full of turkeys for the guys and then is told, "That will be $290.65." It's then, the fun—and embarrassment—begins. It's all caught on tape and shown on the Packer TV show! Did Michels get bamboozled?

"When I was back at USC, my friends who had gone on to the Packers said, 'Oh, we got stuck this year! Our team sent us out to get some free turkeys, and we wound up being the turkeys.' I kind of always remembered that and a little light went on and I said, 'Maybe I won't show up for this one.'"

I asked Timmerman to forgive me for not tipping him off during a show the year before. "Ken would probably have killed me if I had told you."

"No one from South Dakota State warned me, so I got caught hook, line, and sinker. But thanks for not telling me, Steve," he said facetiously. "It would have taken the fun right out of it!"

"It was risky for me to bring it up," I confessed.

"We'll talk later," threatened Timmerman with a grin.

"I'm feeling fine," I told the audience. "I have no thoughts of suicide, so if you find me floating in some gravel pit somewhere and you see a Chevy truck leaving the scene, you'll know, okay? Somebody have the D.A. dig up a tape of this show!"

We tried quickly to make restitution for Adam by talking about his newfound stardom and how it's affected his relationship with his family and friends back home in the northwestern Iowa town of Cherokee.

"Adam, what does happen when you go home?"

"Well, you know, being the grand marshall of the Memorial Day parade," he joked.

Michels also tried to make his way back into Timmerman's graces after the earlier jab. "Is your name up on the water tower yet?"

"No, they still have the name of the town up there, but we're working on it. We're still saving up for the paint. Actually, it's fun to go home and see everybody."

Then it turned into a serious conversation, for a change, when the guys talked about how fame has forced them to adjust to their new life of guarding their phone numbers and speaking platforms. John admitted that he was excited about all the invitations, but then quickly burned himself out. We asked the guys what happens when they forget to acknowledge God's place in their lives.

Adam said, "First of all, you have to give God the credit. He's the one who gave you the talent, and He gave you the family who helped you to work hard to get where you have got. After the games when we kneel down and pray, it puts it all back into perspective."

John Michels made some comments about the pressure put on players who have passed through the intersection of Oneida and Lombardi streets into Lambeau Field. I found it very interesting and convicting.

"It can be really hard because I think a lot of people in this community treat Packers as if they were gods," John said.

I had been waiting for one of the guys to say this for a long time.

"You get in here and you hear how great you are and that you're the greatest thing that's ever happened in this town," he continued.

"And you start believing it," I prodded. He didn't need more motivation to continue.

"You do, you start to listen to it. After the third, fourth, and fifty-third, and hundreth person tells you how great you are, you start thinking, 'Hey, you know, I'm not so bad.' But you can't buy it."

John agreed with Timmerman on one key point. Maybe you had to be there to know how sincere he was when he made this statement. You might be able to get some sense of it here.

"After the game when you 'take a knee,' you are just putting things back in perspective and acknowledging that you're playing the game for one reason. And that's because God gave me the ability. He can take it away it any time. So, I have to use every chance I get to glorify Him and remember why I'm out here playing."

I went on to make the point that these guys have problems just like the rest of us. "Adam," I said, "make us feel like you're like the rest of us."

"I got mustard all over my pants at the pre-game meal. We just moved into a house recently. And husband and wife relations are the same. John, you'll find that out shortly." The room erupted into laughter.

He was giving some advice to the groom-to-be sitting next to him who was scheduled to go down the aisle in February of 1997. At press time, he and Melissa are surviving.

"You know, it's interesting, I don't think people look at what we do as having a job," pointed out Michels. Now, I was a bit confused and a bit serious when I asked, "You mean you guys have jobs? You just play games, football, seasonal, part-time." That had been my line with Ruettgers all the time. He loved it and I knew it would hit home with these guys, as well.

Michels gave us a little more insight into just what it's like to go to his "office."

"I have to go to work, and I have a boss and he's watching over me every day. I make mistakes at work and I get screamed at. There are days I come home and I'm ticked off because I just got my rear end chewed out for something I'd done."

Timmerman sort of giggled in agreement as John continued.

"We go home and we have to deal with the same stuff as everybody else. Maybe even an extra sense of exhaustion because we're running around all day and hitting 300-pound people."

Timmerman took the conversation and the topic to a new level that might have offended, if one didn't know how soft he really is. "When somebody else messes up, let's say they are working at Fort Howard, or whatever, they make a mistake and do something wrong it can stay there, but when we make a mistake, it's in the paper."

I reinforced his point. "Not only is it in the paper, but you get your quarterback smeared and he makes a lot of money. If you allow that to happen too many times, well, it causes problems. It's a wild circle."

John Michels then brought in a term and theory that I never recall hearing in all my days at Campbellsport High School. Well, I admit I didn't pay much attention to anything there, but that's beside the point. John said, "It's the 'Tom Lovat Syndrome.' [Lovat is the Packer offensive line coach.] He's the master of the trickle-down theory. If I take a bad step somewhere, well Alonzo Spellman gets around the corner and hits Brett Favre. Brett's out for the season, we don't go to the playoffs. Everybody gets fired and I lose my job." The next line was pretty scary:

"And the team moves from Green Bay!"

Both guys talked about how important it is for them to share their problems with each other. We can all relate to that. Sometimes the devil tries to tell us we're the only ones who have gone through what we have.

We decided to open up the telephone lines. The first caller was Dave from Neenah. He wanted to know what to tell his ten-year-old son to get through to him the importance of going to church. Michels went first.

"First, I'd say to him, 'How can you have fellowship with a God that you don't know? One of the biggest benefits of going to church is that you get to know Jesus Christ.' I think Eric would find benefit in being around these types of people," he finished.

Just then, without hesitation Timmerman brought to light some wisdom that would have made Reggie jealous. It comforted me, too. "I think you can believe in something without fully understanding it. And at ten years of age he may not understand it. I'm twenty-five years old and I don't understand everything about God. I think it's just a great way to get started."

The conversation eased up a bit as Adam asked Michels if he'd been to the Packer Hall of Fame. John mentioned that he and Derrick Mayes went over there and were throwing passes and kicking field goals, and they got shown up by his fiance!

"So, what's that say for you?" laughed Adam.

"We know where the athletic side of the family will come from," joked the rookie.

I talked about the endorsement possibilites for Michels and he said, "The problem is, between the other offensive lineman, there's nothing left."

"Just scraps," chided Timmerman.

I said something very dangerous then, that increased my chances of getting thrown over a cliff by the burly second-year Iowan.

"Just remember, John, that as a first-round draft choice, your signing bonus, being ten times what John's was, you don't need to be running around with all the menial stuff!"

"Thanks, Steve, I appreciate you starting fires over here," Michels smiled, looking at his teammate.

"Once again, Steve, I appreciate you," joked Timmerman. Great, now I had them both mad at me.

"John, can I wash your car this weekend?" said Adam.

"You know, I suppose we should talk about the football game against the Bears yesterday," I interjected.

But then a caller voiced a concern about prayer being taken off of the field and Timmerman made a good point. "Reggie is leading the prayer and he's pretty popular." We all laughed.

"Mr. White, you and your friends are going to have to leave," I joked.

As I told the caller, Pam, that she had won a copy of my book, and mentioned that it had sold 20,000 copies, I had to put up with a jab from Timmerman.

"They are all in Steve's basement."

"OOOhhh! That hurt, coming from a guy I thought was my friend," I said.

Another caller brought up a good point about how a lot of money can be a doorway to temptation and distraction. John made a really honest, humble point.

"For me, it's the first time in my life that I actually have some money."

"Not like Adam," I said, "who grew up with a golden spoon in his mouth from all those soybeans in Iowa."

"I had to take a pay cut to come here," said Adam.

"John, there's a load of money down there, I'm serious," I said. "Picture Adam after not working out for three months. That's what they all look like down there."

"He's got his Ferrari tractor down there," laughed Michels.

"It's a green and gold John Deere" said Timmerman.

Then the line of the evening came out. I was telling Timmerman how Beebe had joked with me that he was giving Timmerman a rough time about his Chevy commercials. Adam acknowledged that Beebe wasn't the only Packer who was teasing him.

Just who was the other? Well, it was Brett Favre, who is a pitchman for Bergstrom Automotive in Appleton. And Timmerman good-naturedly thought the two-time MVP was the last guy who should be picking on him.

"What's really funny is, Brett tries to give me a hard time—it's like, 'Brett, have you seen your own commercial? It's terrible.'" The place erupted.

In a low voice, Michels mocked Favre's commercial, "Bergstrom, for the love of driving."

"Somebody grab a copy of this and we'll send it to Brett," I threatened.

I couldn't believe both these these guys were bold enough to pick on the man they get paid to protect. Well, maybe Favre would let it slide, knowing he needs that protection.

Timmerman wasn't done with his jabs. "It's like Brett, loosen up a bit. Move your neck. You can turn from side to side a little bit." Then, it occurred to him after his lengthy harangue that there might be repercussions.

"I'll probably regret this. I'll go to work and my locker will be messed up on Wednesday."

"We're gonna can this on a cassette," I said, "And John's gonna hand it to him. John's going to say, 'I wash my hands of this. I was sitting next to him, but I take none of the responsibility for it.'"

"Just remember who's got your blind side, Brett," said Michels. (The blind side is the area of the field Brett cannot see when he's dropping back to pass. He especially needs protection there, and it's often up to the left tackle, the position John plays, to provide that protection.)

As the theme music rolled, indicating that it was time to move on, I reminded the listeners and, prayerfully, the local constabulary, that I had no intentions of jumping off a cliff.

"I'm gonna get framed for this whole thing," Adam replied.

"Just remember folks, there have been threats made to me tonight," I said.

"From Kid Raider," [our producer] laughed Michels.

"So, call the station," joked Timmerman.

It was a wrap. One show I will not forget any time soon.

As I later listened to the interview on tape, I couldn't help but wonder what Michels and Timmerman would have replied, had I asked them if they could have imagined what the next couple of months would bring.

The good news is, I have talked to each since the Super Bowl, and they're still . . . well, as humble as a kid from California and a former Iowa soybean farmer who used to play for the South Dakota State Jack Rabbits. And they're still crazy as ever!

The Leap of Faith Sports Radio Show can be heard on the Winners Success Radio Network. Steve Rose hosts the show with John Michels of the Packers. For the broadcast schedule of the Leap of Faith Sports Radio show station near you, write or call:

Winners Success Radio Network
Box 404-L
Neenah, WI 54957-0404
920 995-2395

RESOURCES

Rawhide Boys Ranch
John and Jan Gillespie, founders
Rawhide Road
New London, WI 54961
920 982-6100

Urban Hope
P.O. Box 11475
Green Bay, WI 54313
(This is Reggie White's relief fund for churches. Tax-deductable contributions are appreciated.)

Donna J. Morgan, licensed therapist
130 Hilly Oak Drive
Delafield, WI 53018
414 646-8520

Reggie's Prayer
636 W. College Avenue
Suite 920
Appleton, WI 54911-5804
(To order a copy of Reggie's Prayer, call toll-free 1-888-783-2405)

Christian Children's Fund
2821 Emerywood Parkway
Box 26484
Richmond, VA 23261-6484

Prairie Oak Press
821 Prospect Place
Madison, WI 53703
(To order more copies of this book, call toll-free 1-888-833-9118. In the 608 area, call 255-2288.)

If this book has personally blessed you or challenged you spiritually, Steve Rose would love for you to write personally and tell him about it. If you have questions about how to become a Christian, or take your relationship with God to the next level, feel free to write or call for information.

Steve Rose
Winners Success Radio Network
P.O. Box 404
Neenah, WI 54957-0404
920 995-2395

All correspondence will be answered as quickly as possible. You are very important to Steve, and you are the reason this book was written. When we hear from you, you can know that Reggie White, Robert Brooks, and the other believers will be praying for you.

On behalf of all of us, God Bless You, friend.

Mike Utech
Winners Success Radio Network